BILL'S EVERYDA

Bi

BILL'S EVERYDAY ASIAN

Bill Granger

Photography by Mikkel Vang

quadrille

I underestimated how much of a trip down memory lane it would be for me when I started writing this book.

From an early age, growing up in Australia, the influence of Asian flavours have inspired me and shaped the way I look at cooking and eating like nothing else: from visiting the Chinese restaurant owned by my best friend's family when I was eight years old, to the exotic, heady scent that wafted from barbecues and street vendors while I was travelling in Indonesia in my late teens, and memories of partying in Koh Phangan in my twenties – while everyone was on the beach eating egg and chips I'd be watching a toothless old lady making buffalo curries and green papaya salads in a tiny, hutlike kitchen. All those big, bold, salty, sour, sweet and spicy taste explosions had me hooked and have never released their grip, always spurring me on to try more.

Although these experiences may not apply to everyone, most people I meet, wherever they're from, remember their first brushes with the vibrant flavours of Asia. And over the years, as we've become more well-travelled, these flavours have infiltrated our food culture more and more, permeating through in all sorts of wild and wonderful, and sometimes questionable ways; from salads and lunchtime wraps and pizzas to sweet chilli everything!

With this book I wanted to draw on all my encounters to demystify the idea that preparing this kind of food is more complicated than anything else – in a lot of cases it's so much simpler. The secret is in the balance; achieving harmony between salty (soy, fish sauce), sweet (brown sugar, honey), sour (lime) and hot (chilli) with some help from aromatics like ginger, garlic, coriander and lemon grass. You'll know when you get it right. And the best part is, in most cases, you only need one wok or pan to create the most delicious meal.

If you think about it, preparing simple Italian food has become something most of us hardly think about any more. If you've got the basics – olive oil, garlic, lemons, perhaps a little chilli and good fresh ingredients – you're good to go. The best way to approach Asian food is by looking at it in exactly the same way. The principles are surprisingly similar; you can even substitute the pasta for noodles.

I've had numerous food crushes, from Moroccan to Lebanese, Provençal to Tuscan, and enjoy throwing ingredients together in all manner of ways – I'd get bored if I only stuck to one cuisine – but, for me, Asian food transcends trends; it's about clear, fresh flavours that make absolute sense together and excite the palate every time.

It's about healthy, zingy, uplifting dishes that can be prepared quickly and easily – plus a few that are marinated and cooked slowly to enhance those deeply savoury flavours, but are just as simple to make. My one rule is that nothing should require a list of a hundred hard-to-find ingredients or be swimming in gunky, unidentifiable sauce. I'm particularly passionate about Thai and Vietnamese salads, usually with a good kick of citrus and chilli, but working in Japan I've become increasingly interested in the more refined nuances of flavour you find there. Apart from chicken sashimi (although not as terrifying as it sounds), I think I can safely say that I've yet to find an Asian dish I don't like.

The dishes I've chosen to include in this book are inspired by all my taste adventures, from the simplest, businessman's breakfast in Tokyo to a home-cooked dinner I enjoyed in Singapore, along with some of the most exciting things I've tried in restaurants around the world.

I hope you enjoy experimenting, cooking and, of course, eating everything as much as I have.

BILL'S ASIAN PANTRY

For those of you who know me it probably won't come as a big surprise to learn that I'm not a great believer in using a million 'essential' ingredients, even for Asian-style cooking. I've been through the phase of wanting to be authentic down to the last detail but, these days, I'm a lot more mellow. If you're in an 'obsessive foodie' phase – which, by the way, there's nothing wrong with, love every minute when I'm there – then please, be my guest and trawl round your closest Chinatown looking for lotus root and lily buds. But otherwise the following list should carry you happily through most of the recipes in this book.

BILL'S ASIAN PANTRY

Balsamic vinegar
This kitchen staple works perfectly well as a substitute for Chinese black vinegar.

Bamboo shoots
A classic ingredient that's always good to have a couple of jars or tins of in your cupboard to add extra texture to stir-fries.

Bonito flakes
Dried and smoked bonito fish, used widely by the Japanese in dashi and as a garnish.

Chilli – oil, dried flakes & fresh
I do like a kick of chilli, so I always have it in several different forms because they all bring their own variation to a dish.

Chinese chilli sauce
Unlike the sweet and sticky Thai version, this spicy and savoury sauce is one of the classic dim sum dipping sauces served at Chinese restaurants. Sriracha sauce can be used as an alternative.

Chinese five spice powder
An aromatic all-purpose seasoning that you'll find yourself using in a multitude of dishes.

Cinnamon sticks
I much prefer using a cinnamon stick in a curry to impart that lovely sweet flavour rather than the ready-ground sort.

Coconut milk
Remember to freeze any leftover coconut milk you have in ice-cube trays to add to recipes in the future.

Curry paste
It's fun to make your own curry paste at least once – I have included my recipe (see page 115) – but for every day, shop-bought red, green and yellow pastes are a great kitchen short cut to have in your cupboard.

Dashi powder
Seriously, life is too short to make this bonito and kombu stock from scratch – well, for me, anyway. Take a tip from Japanese home cooks and make life easier by using the instant powder version.

Fish sauce
I couldn't be without this for creating zingy Thai dressings and anything that needs a kick of umami.

Garlic
Forget the tubes of paste and jars of 'cheat's garlic'. As much as I'm a fan of a short cut, there's nothing like the fresh stuff. And throw out your garlic crusher too if you still have one.

Ginger
This root can dry out quickly, even when kept in the fridge, so buy in fairly small quantities and use immediately.

Hoisin sauce
Rich and dark, this traditional sauce coats everything in its path with its delicious and deeply savoury-sweet glaze.

Lemon grass
There's no substitute for fresh lemon grass – it immediately imparts the scent and taste of Asia to everything you use it in.

Light-flavoured oil
Although flavours tend to be pretty strong with Asian cuisine, it's always good to use a cooking oil that's light in both consistency and taste. I usually reach for rapeseed oil or good old-fashioned sunflower oil.

Mirin
A light, sweet rice wine that adds a touch of mellowness to soy dressings and marinades.

Miso paste
Classic red miso paste can be used in both soups and stews, while white miso paste is a deliciously rich and buttery marinade for white fish, aubergine and other vegetable dishes.

Noodles – egg, rice noodles (fine & wide), buckwheat soba
A good stock of noodles is essential as they're incredibly versatile and will save the day, or evening, on many occasions.

Nori

These sheets of dried seaweed are traditionally used to wrap sushi rolls and are delicious shredded over steamed rice.

Nuoc cham

Related to Thai 'nahm jim', this is a potent mix of fish sauce, sugar and lime to which aromatics such as garlic, chilli and ginger can be added. To make your own, pound 1 garlic clove with 1 de-seeded and roughly chopped red chilli and a pinch of sea salt. Add 2 tablespoons fish sauce, 3 tablespoons lime juice and 1 tablespoon caster sugar and mix well.

Oyster sauce

Almost as essential as soy sauce, the fishy yet mellow saltiness of this condiment adds depth mainly to Chinese dishes.

Panko

As much as I like to try to cook wholesome there's no substitute for these light, feathery Japanese breadcrumbs. I'm not sure how much real bread is involved but the result is almost tempura-like.

Rice – basmati, coconut, jasmine & brown

As long as you have rice in the pantry, you have a meal. Once you've mastered making the perfect rice (see page 199), you'll be showing off your skills every night.

Rice vinegar

This is sweeter and softer than white wine vinegar, which makes it perfect for Asian cooking.

Sambal oelek

This is an intensely spicy and popular Indonesian chilli sauce that includes the seeds of the chillies and is more of a relish rather than a paste. Great for that extra heat hit, which I love.

Sesame oil

The unique smoky nuttiness of this oil adds an additional flavour layer to sauces and marinades. I particularly like the Japanese variety.

Shaoxing (Chinese rice) wine

This wine is used liberally in a number of Chinese dishes. Unless you're a connoisseur, buy the cooking version. Dry sherry is a good substitute.

Soy sauce

Whether you prefer light soy, classic soy, shoyu or tamari, it's good to have both the light and dark options in your store cupboard.

Star anise

This must be just about my favourite aromatic spice. It cries out to be used in so many Asian dishes I make.

Sweet chilli sauce

My daughter Edie wouldn't be without this to dip her chips in. Most people use it for spring rolls and other crispy fried appetisers though. I make mine by combining 3 finely diced large red chillies, 250ml rice vinegar, 2 teaspoons sea salt, 185g caster sugar and 2 chopped garlic cloves in a small saucepan over medium–high heat. Bring to the boil, reduce the heat and simmer until reduced by half. Cool before serving.

Tamarind paste

A distinctively sweet-sour ingredient which can't really be substituted. If pushed, however, a combination of lime juice and soft brown sugar is the closest you can get to the real thing.

Tofu

Love it or hate it, I can't tell you how many last-minute cooking dilemmas that having both silken and firm tofu in your fridge will solve.

Wasabi paste

Japan's answer to horseradish, this spicy green paste adds a kick to many more dishes than sushi.

Water chestnuts

On a similar note to bamboo shoots, water chestnuts give a lovely distinctive and authentic crunch to many Chinese dishes.

Starters

It's almost impossible to think of Asian food without thinking of the appetisers. All those irresistible crispy, crunchy parcels and steamed, taste-packed little morsels you get at the beginning of a meal that are so satisfying in themselves it can be hard to leave room for the rest. The heady scent of Thai fishcakes and crispy wontons – with sweet chilli sauce, of course (preferably home-made) – gets my mouth watering every time, but I also adore the less guilty pleasure and fresher flavours that summer rolls and simply seared tuna tataki offer – the perfect balance of texture, taste and all-important raw crunch. But what I love most about Asian snacks and starters is that they're made for sharing. What could be more perfect with drinks than bowls of spicy almonds and cashews and golden beef curry puffs, straight from the oven? My kids can never resist any kind of sticky chicken wings. And me? I'm addicted to pickles – the Eastern alternative to olives. These intensely flavoursome small bites are surprisingly easy to throw together yourself, and are the ideal finger food for both formal and informal gatherings – even if you don't manage to make anything else! They also remind me of some of the first street food I ever tried in Asia, so it's safe to say they'll always have a special place in my heart.

Prawn, ginger & spring onion wontons

Deep-frying doesn't have to mean having a huge vat of oil bubbling away on the stovetop – with these you need just enough oil to cover them to make them crisp and golden. I like to serve them as a prelude to a light meal, with a cold glass of something sparkling.

500g raw prawns, peeled, de-veined
   and chopped
1 tablespoon chopped coriander leaves
2 spring onions, finely chopped
1 teaspoon grated ginger
1 tablespoon oyster sauce
1 teaspoon sesame oil
24 wonton wrappers
light-flavoured oil, for frying
soy and chilli dipping sauce
   (see recipe below)

Mix together the prawns, coriander, spring onion, ginger, oyster sauce and sesame oil. Put a wonton wrapper on the work surface, place a teaspoonful of filling in the middle, run a wet finger around the edge of the wrapper and then fold it in half to make a triangle. Seal the edges, then fold the top two points of the triangle down over each other to make a shape like a tortellini.

Heat the oil in a deep fryer or frying pan over medium heat and deep-fry or shallow-fry the wontons in batches for 2 minutes or until golden. Drain on kitchen paper and serve immediately with the dipping sauce. **Makes 24**

Soy & chilli dipping sauce
4 tablespoons soy sauce
4 tablespoons rice vinegar
½ teaspoon chilli oil
1 teaspoon sesame oil
2 spring onions, finely sliced

Mix together the soy sauce, vinegar, chilli oil, sesame oil and spring onion. Set aside.

Quick cucumber pickles

It's funny how we all love buying cookbooks but from some of them we might only make one or two recipes. In the early nineties I was a big fan of the late Barbara Tropp, who owned China Moon in San Francisco, but have to admit, the only thing I ever made from her book more than once was the super-easy cucumber pickles. Call me lazy.

3 tablespoons rice vinegar
1 tablespoon caster sugar
3 tablespoons soy sauce
1 teaspoon sesame oil
½ teaspoon dried chilli flakes
4 small cucumbers, cut into chunks

Combine the vinegar, sugar, soy sauce, sesame oil and chilli flakes in a large bowl. Add the cucumbers and toss to mix. Cover and leave to marinate in the fridge for 1 hour, stirring occasionally. **Serves 6**

Nuts three ways

When my wife Natalie was working on a documentary in China, she loved that the waiters always brought a little plate of plain roasted peanuts to the table before each meal instead of bread. Whatever kind of food you're serving, a few salty-sweet or spicy oven-roasted nuts never go amiss with pre-dinner drinks and they fill the house with a lovely toasty aroma.

Spice-crusted almonds

200g whole blanched almonds
1 egg white, lightly whisked
100g granulated sugar
½ teaspoon sea salt
½ teaspoon ground cinnamon
1 teaspoon ground cumin
1 teaspoon ground paprika
½ teaspoon chilli flakes

Preheat the oven to 160°C/gas mark 2–3. Lightly oil a baking tray. Toss the almonds in egg white. Combine the sugar, salt and spices in a bowl and add the almonds. Spread the nuts out in an even layer on the tray and bake for 20–25 minutes. Leave to cool before breaking up to serve. **Serves 8**

Maple tamari cashews

200g raw cashews
2 teaspoons tamari
2 teaspoons maple syrup
½ teaspoon Chinese five spice powder

Preheat the oven to 180°C/gas mark 4. Line a baking tray with foil. Spread the nuts out on the tray and bake for 15 minutes or until golden. Combine the tamari, maple syrup and five spice powder in a bowl. Add the warm nuts and toss to coat. Spread the nuts out on the tray once again and return to the oven for 3–5 minutes. Leave to cool before serving. **Serves 8**

Lime-roasted peanuts

375g raw peanuts
1½ tablespoons lime juice
1½ tablespoons olive oil
1 tablespoon hot paprika
1 tablespoon sea salt
1 teaspoon freshly ground black pepper

Preheat the oven to 180°C/gas mark 4. Line a baking tray with foil. Spread the nuts out on the tray. Combine the lime juice, olive oil, hot paprika, salt and pepper, drizzle over the nuts and toss well. Bake for 15 minutes, shaking occasionally, until golden and toasted. Serve warm or cold. **Serves 6**

Summary rolls with a peanut dipping sauce

We had the ultimate fusion Christmas party at bills one year when we served French St Germain elderflower liqueur with Tasmanian Sauvignon Blanc, San Pellegrino and trays of Vietnamese summer rolls for everyone to make themselves. Here's the basic method and some suggestions for fillings.

300g rice vermicelli
375g (pack of 40) 22cm round rice paper wrappers
peanut dipping sauce (see recipe below)

suggested fillings
duck, cucumber and watercress:
 cooked and shredded duck breast,
 cucumber batons and watercress
firm tofu, avocado and coriander:
 cooked and sliced tofu, avocado slices
 and coriander leaves
prawn, mango and coriander:
 cooked, peeled and de-veined prawns,
 mango slices and coriander

Place the rice vermicelli in a bowl and pour in enough boiling water to cover. Soak for 3–4 minutes, then drain and refresh under cold running water before draining thoroughly. Place on a serving dish.

Place a large bowl of hot water on the table to soak the rice paper wrappers. Arrange the fillings on a serving platter (suggestions above) alongside the rice vermicelli, the wrappers and the peanut dipping sauce.

To make the summer rolls, soften your rice paper wrapper in the hot water for 30 seconds–1 minute then shake off any excess water. Place the wrapper on a plate, top with a little vermicelli and the filling of your choice and roll up, flipping the ends over first and then tucking in the sides. **Makes 40**

Peanut dipping sauce
2 teaspoons light-flavoured oil
2 garlic cloves, finely chopped
1 large red chilli, finely diced
2 tablespoons smooth peanut butter
125ml hoisin sauce
2 tablespoons Chinese chilli sauce
2 teaspoons soft brown sugar

Heat the oil in a small saucepan over medium heat. Add the garlic and chilli and cook for 2 minutes. Whisk in 125ml water, the peanut butter, hoisin sauce, chilli sauce and sugar and bring to the boil. Cook for a further minute. Leave to cool.

Tuna tataki

This seared tuna dish has become a restaurant staple. It's the perfect compromise when you want a sashimi fix at home as you don't need to be so exact with the preparation but you still get that great, fresh clean-tasting flavour. It's also a sure-fire hit with guys wanting to make dinner for their girlfriends for the first time.

1 tablespoon grated ginger
1½ tablespoons sesame seeds
1 tablespoon freshly ground black pepper
250g very fresh tuna
1 tablespoon light-flavoured oil, for frying
4 spring onions, cut into 5cm batons
1 tablespoon soy sauce
1 tablespoon mirin
1 lime, cut in half to serve

In a shallow bowl, mix together the ginger, sesame seeds and pepper. Season the tuna with sea salt to taste then coat the tuna completely in the ginger mixture.

Preheat a large frying pan over high heat. Add the oil and cook the tuna for 30 seconds on each of the four sides. Remove from the pan and set aside to cool.

Slice the tuna thinly and serve with the spring onion batons, the combined soy sauce and mirin for dipping and the lime. **Serves 4**

Sticky sesame chicken wings

These are inspired by Nagoya in Japan, which is famous for its restaurants that serve nothing but chicken wings; from sticky and sweet to lip-numbingly spicy. They're such a universal guilty pleasure, I must admit I've had visions of starting a Bill's Chicken Wings chain myself.

1.5kg chicken wings
1 tablespoon light-flavoured oil
3 garlic cloves, crushed with
   the flat of a knife
1 long red chilli, finely chopped
4 tablespoons mirin
4 tablespoons soy sauce
4 tablespoons sake
110g granulated sugar
1½ tablespoons sesame seeds,
   toasted (optional)

Preheat the oven to 200°C/gas mark 6. Line a large roasting tray with non-stick baking paper. Place the wings in the tray and roast for 35–40 minutes or until starting to brown. Meanwhile, heat the oil in a medium-sized saucepan over medium–high heat. Add the garlic and chilli and cook for 1–2 minutes or until the garlic is turning golden. Add the mirin, soy sauce, sake and sugar and cook for 5 minutes or until the liquid has reduced by half.

Remove the chicken from the oven and pour over the sticky mirin mixture. Toss to coat and return to the oven, basting occasionally, for a further 15–20 minutes. If desired, scatter with sesame seeds to serve. **Serves 8**

Curry puffs

Inspired by the venison curry puffs at Yauatcha, one of my favourite Chinese restaurants in London, these will always have a special significance as I made them when my youngest daughter Bunny was going through a particularly fussy phase of not liking anything that was put in front of her at mealtimes. She loved these little puffs, however, and is always asking me when I'm going to make them again.

150g peeled potato, finely chopped
1½ tablespoons light-flavoured oil
1 small onion, finely chopped
1½ tablespoons finely grated ginger
2 garlic cloves, crushed with
    the flat of a knife
2 teaspoons medium-hot curry powder
150g chicken breast, finely chopped
80g frozen peas
small handful coriander leaves, chopped
about 5 sheets ready-rolled puff pastry,
    thawed (for 25 x 10cm rounds)
1 egg, lightly beaten
2 tablespoons sesame seeds
Chinese chilli sauce

Place the potato in boiling salted water for 10 minutes, then drain. Heat the oil in a large frying pan over medium heat. Add the onion, ginger and garlic and cook for 5 minutes or until softened. Add the curry powder and cook, stirring constantly, for 20 seconds. Add the chicken and cooked potato, increase the heat to medium–high and cook, stirring, for 2–3 minutes or until the chicken is just cooked. Add the frozen peas, take off the heat and set aside to cool. When cool, stir in the coriander and season with sea salt and freshly ground black pepper to taste. Preheat the oven to 190°C/gas mark 5.

Cut 25 x 10cm rounds from the pastry sheets. Lightly brush around the edge of the pastry rounds with water and place 1 flat tablespoon of the mixture on each. Fold up to make a half-moon shape, then place on a baking paper lined baking sheet and press the edges together with a fork. Brush with egg and top with sesame seeds. Repeat with the remaining pastry. (It's better to have only a few rounds of pastry out of the fridge at a time.)

Bake for 15–20 minutes or until crisp and golden. Serve with Chinese chilli sauce. **Makes 25**

Fishcakes just refuse
to go out of fashion.
And what's not to love
about these tasty,
spicy little patties?

Thai fishcakes

Fishcakes are a perennial favourite and this version is a great crowd-pleaser. Shallow-fried in just a little oil, I guarantee the ones you make at home will not only taste better but will be healthier than anything you eat in a restaurant.

500g boneless, skinless,
    fleshy white fish, roughly chopped
3 tablespoons red curry paste
1 teaspoon granulated sugar
2 tablespoons fish sauce
6 kaffir lime leaves, very finely sliced,
    or finely grated zest of 2 limes
60g snake beans or green beans,
    very thinly sliced
80ml light-flavoured oil
cucumber relish (see recipe below)

Blend the fish in a food processor until smooth, scraping the sides down once or twice. Add the curry paste and pulse with the sugar, fish sauce and lime leaves.

Scrape into a large bowl, add the snake beans and stir to combine. Take a handful of the mixture and throw against the side of the bowl to firm the proteins, repeating a few times until the mixture is noticeably firmer.

With moistened hands, form slightly heaped tablespoonfuls of the mixture into discs. Heat the oil in a large non-stick frying pan over medium heat and fry in batches until browned and cooked through. Drain on kitchen paper and serve hot with the cucumber relish. **Makes 24**

Cucumber relish
125ml rice vinegar or white vinegar
125g caster sugar
1 small cucumber, quartered
    lengthways and finely sliced
½ tablespoon finely julienned ginger
1 large red chilli, de-seeded and finely sliced

Place the vinegar and sugar in a small saucepan over medium heat and stir until the sugar has dissolved. Remove from the heat and cool. Pour into a bowl, add the cucumber, ginger and chilli and stir to combine.

Two dips

A great alternative to the usual taco chips and guacamole combo, the creamy smoothness of the avocado contrasts perfectly with the heat of the wasabi and the crunch of some shop-bought rice crackers or a plate of crudités. The deliciously savoury aubergine dip always makes me think of the izakayas in Japan, which are a bit like tapas bars and where they serve the most enormous cold glasses of beer.

Miso & aubergine dip

2 medium aubergines (about 350g each)
2 tablespoons light-flavoured oil
2 tablespoons white miso paste
1 tablespoon soy sauce
1 tablespoon lime juice
1 garlic clove, crushed with the flat of a knife
1 teaspoon caster sugar
1 tablespoon sesame seeds, toasted
1 carrot, cut into long wedges and cut in
    half crossways at an angle
1 cucumber, cut into long wedges and cut
    in half crossways at an angle

Preheat the oven to 200°C/gas mark 6. Halve the aubergines lengthways, score and place on a baking tray lined with foil and brush with the oil. Roast for 45 minutes or until slightly charred and soft. Scoop the flesh out of the skin. Place in a food processor with the miso paste, soy sauce, lime juice, garlic and sugar and pulse until smooth. Place in a serving dish, sprinkle with sesame seeds and serve with carrot and cucumber wedges for dipping. **Serves 6**

Avocado dip with wasabi

2 ripe avocados, peeled and diced
4 spring onions, finely chopped
1 tablespoon lemon juice
½ teaspoon wasabi paste
1 tablespoon mirin
2 teaspoons soy sauce
rice crackers

Place the avocado and spring onion in a bowl. Put the lemon juice, wasabi paste, mirin and soy sauce in another small bowl and stir to combine. Add the dressing to the avocado and spring onion and stir with a fork to combine, keeping some of the texture. Spoon into a serving dish and serve with rice crackers. **Serves 6**

Soups

Inspired by my mum's cookery magazines, the first thing I ever learnt to cook as a child was Chinese-style sweetcorn soup using tinned creamed corn. Then, when I went to Japan when I was 18 or 19 and living on a shoestring, I learnt to rely on great steaming bowls of the cheapest kind of miso ramen. But it was probably on a trip to Indonesia in my early twenties, when I saw taxi drivers and airline staff eating spicy noodle soups at the airport for breakfast that I became truly converted to the idea of just how satisfying those one-bowl meals could be. When I got back to Sydney I went in search of the best noodle places. The bowls of the full monty (with liver, kidneys and all) were too much for me, so I'd always go for plain chicken or beef. Restorative and satisfying, Asian soups in all their forms are a great thing to make to get the family slurping along together. Just remember to invest in large bowls!

Rice noodle pho with rare beef & star anise

A lean, mean, satisfying soup, this is a great way to make good-quality steak go a bit further. Non-traditionally, I like to add a few vegetables for crunch and the noodles give you that wonderful slippery, slurpy texture. The perfect one-bowl dinner.

1 tablespoon soy sauce
1 tablespoon honey
2 tablespoons fish sauce
2 sirloin steaks (about 300g each),
    fat removed
375g rice noodles
1 litre chicken stock
5 slices ginger
2 tablespoons lime juice
1 cinnamon stick
2 teaspoons granulated sugar
3 star anise
1 tablespoon light-flavoured oil
1 bunch bok choy,
    leaves cut in long strips
1 red chilli, sliced
handful Thai basil leaves

Put the soy sauce, honey, half the fish sauce and a pinch of sea salt in a shallow dish and stir to combine. Add the steak, cover the dish and leave to marinate for 5 minutes.

Meanwhile, place the rice noodles in a large bowl, cover with boiling water and leave to soak according to the instructions on the packet. Drain and refresh under cold running water.

Place the stock, 500ml water, ginger, lime juice, the remaining fish sauce, cinnamon stick, sugar and the star anise in a medium-sized saucepan. Bring to the boil, then reduce the heat and simmer for 5 minutes.

Heat a large frying pan over medium–high heat for 2 minutes, add the oil and sear the steaks for 2 minutes on each side. Remove from the pan and allow to rest for 2 minutes.

Divide the noodles and bok choy between four serving bowls. Ladle the hot soup into the bowls and top with sliced steak, red chilli slices and basil leaves. **Serves 4**

Satisfying and
restorative, Asian
soups are not
just a prelude to
a meal but often
the main event.

Sweetcorn soup

*When you don't want something
that slaps you around the face
with spices and heat, or you need
something more kid-friendly,
this comforting, creamy, golden
soup always hits the spot.
You can't beat the earthy taste
of fresh corn but I won't tell
if you cheat with the frozen or
tinned kind.*

2 tablespoons light-flavoured oil
8 spring onions, white and green parts
   separated and chopped
2 garlic cloves, crushed with the flat of a knife
2 tablespoons finely chopped ginger
600g corn kernels, cut from the cob
   (about 6 cobs)
1 litre chicken or vegetable stock
3 eggs, lightly beaten
2 tablespoons soy sauce
1 teaspoon sesame oil
3 tablespoons mirin

Heat the oil in a large saucepan over medium–high heat. Add
the white spring onion, garlic and ginger and cook for 2–3 minutes.
Add the corn and stock and 500ml water, bring to the boil
then reduce to a simmer and cook for 20 minutes or until the
corn is tender.

Purée half the soup and return to the pan. Pour in the eggs in a
thin stream, stirring constantly. Add the soy sauce, sesame
oil and mirin and season with sea salt and freshly ground black
pepper to taste. Ladle into serving bowls and dress with the
spring onion greens. **Serves 4**

Roast chicken & egg noodle soup

*I'm always looking for new ways
to use leftover chicken and
with this take on a classic I've
added orange, cinnamon
and star anise to deepen and
enrich the flavour, and sprinkled
a few shredded leeks on top
– making it perfect for a chilly,
autumn day or evening.*

1 litre chicken stock
3 tablespoons soy sauce
1 teaspoon caster sugar
2 star anise
2 cinnamon sticks
2 strips orange peel
2 tablespoons mirin or dry sherry
250g dried thin egg noodles
300g Chinese broccoli,
   cut in half and blanched
½ barbecued (rotisserie) chicken,
   skin removed and meat shredded
1 small leek, shredded
2 teaspoons sesame oil

Place the stock, 1 litre water, soy sauce, sugar, star anise,
cinnamon sticks, orange peel and mirin in a large saucepan and
bring to the boil. Remove from heat. Meanwhile, cook the
noodles according to the instructions on the packet. Drain and
refresh under cold running water.

Divide the noodles, Chinese broccoli and chicken between
four bowls. Pour over the hot soup and finish with the shredded
leek, a drizzle of sesame oil and season with freshly ground
black pepper. **Serves 4**

Chicken, mushroom & coconut soup

For anyone who worries about the calorific content of coconut milk in Asian food, let me reassure you that, although some restaurants might use litres of the stuff, when cooking at home you only ever really need a dash. The coconut milk will enhance this lovely chicken and lemon grass stock beautifully.

200ml coconut milk
500ml chicken stock
3cm piece ginger, peeled and sliced
2 lemon grass stalks, cut into 5cm pieces
    and whacked with the flat of a knife
5 kaffir lime leaves or 3 strips lime peel
400g skinless chicken breasts or thighs
200g mixed Asian mushrooms
2 tablespoons lime juice
2 tablespoons fish sauce
1 tablespoon caster sugar
handful baby spinach leaves, finely sliced

Put the coconut milk, chicken stock, 500ml water, ginger, lemon grass and lime leaves in a saucepan and bring to the boil. Reduce the heat to low, add the chicken and simmer for 7 minutes. Add the mushrooms and simmer for a further 3 minutes. Add the lime juice, fish sauce and sugar and remove from the heat.

Lift the chicken from the soup and cut into chunks. Place in each serving bowl, top with the spinach leaves and mushrooms from the pan, then ladle the soup over the top. **Serves 4**

Chicken curry soup

This is the antidote to a grey, wintery day when you need a bit of colour and spice in your life. Fragrant, comforting and just sinus-clearing enough, it's Asia's cure-all broth and I've yet to meet anyone who doesn't agree.

1 tablespoon light-flavoured oil
3 garlic cloves, finely sliced
1 lemon grass stalk, white part cut into 3 sections
1½ tablespoons curry powder
750ml chicken stock
400ml tin coconut milk
2 tablespoons fish sauce
1 tablespoon caster sugar
400g orange sweet potato
2 chicken breast fillets (about 500g)
1 bunch Chinese broccoli, leaves only
250g small rice stick noodles (soaked in
    boiling water, drained and rinsed)
1 red chilli, finely sliced
½ small red onion, cut into thin wedges
2 tablespoons crispy shallots

Heat the oil in a medium-sized saucepan over medium heat. Add the garlic and lemon grass and cook, stirring, until golden. Add the curry powder and continue stirring for 30 seconds. Add the stock, 750ml water, coconut milk, fish sauce and caster sugar. Reduce the heat to a simmer. Peel the sweet potato, cut into chunks and add to the soup. Poach gently for 5 minutes. Add the chicken and continue to poach for another 8 minutes.

Take the pan off the heat and set aside to rest for 5 minutes, adding the Chinese broccoli in the final 2 minutes. Remove the chicken and slice. Place the noodles in four noodle bowls, cover with the chicken and soup and dress with the red chilli, onion wedges and crispy shallots. **Serves 4**

Duck soup

When I first opened bills in Sydney, I would often go to a Thai restaurant in the backstreets of the industrial quarter for lunch. My friend would have the 'boat soup', which was too dark and bloody for me. I preferred the subtlety of the star anise-scented duck broth which, though rich and satisfying, was a little more refined.

150g vermicelli noodles
4 spring onions, chopped into 5cm pieces
3cm piece ginger, peeled and sliced
1 tablespoon fish sauce
1 tablespoon caster sugar
2 star anise
2 duck breasts (about 420g),
    skin removed
¼ Chinese cabbage, shredded
¼ pineapple, peeled
    and cut into small pieces
4 spring onions,
    finely sliced on the diagonal
handful coriander leaves
handful mint leaves
1 red chilli, sliced

Soak the noodles in hot water for 2 minutes to soften, then drain well. Put 1.5 litres water, the chopped spring onion, ginger, fish sauce, sugar and star anise in a large saucepan and bring to the boil. Add the duck breasts, reduce the heat to a simmer and poach the duck gently for 2 minutes.

Take the pan off the heat, cover with a lid and leave to stand for 15 minutes. Remove the duck from the pan and allow to cool slightly, then shred the meat. Strain the liquid and reheat.

Divide the vermicelli noodles, shredded duck, cabbage and pineapple between four large noodle bowls. Ladle over the soup and serve topped with the spring onion, coriander and mint leaves and red chilli. **Serves 4**

Butternut squash, chilli & coconut soup

I had an unfortunate incident once with an enormous pumpkin we'd had on display at one of the restaurants and then put out the back and forgotten about. I won't put you off by going into any more detail, but I wish I'd had this recipe at the time as, instead of wasting the pumpkin, I could have made a freezerful of this smooth, creamy soup. Rather than use the garlic and dried spices you could also try making this with a heaped tablespoon of red curry paste.

2 tablespoons light-flavoured oil
3 garlic cloves, roughly chopped
1 red chilli, chopped
1 teaspoon ground cumin
1 teaspoon ground coriander
1 teaspoon ground cinnamon
1 tablespoon paprika
1kg butternut squash, peeled,
   de-seeded and chopped
2 carrots, roughly chopped
200ml coconut milk
3 tablespoons fish sauce
2 tablespoons lime juice, to taste
extra coconut milk, to drizzle
1 red chilli, finely sliced on an angle
2 tablespoons chopped coriander leaves

Heat the oil in a medium-sized saucepan. Add the garlic and spices and cook over medium heat for 1 minute until fragrant. Add the butternut squash and carrot and cook, stirring, over medium heat for a further minute.

Add 1.5 litres water and bring to the boil, then reduce the heat and simmer for 25–30 minutes or until the vegetables are soft. Cool slightly and purée until smooth. Add the coconut milk, fish sauce and lime juice and season with sea salt to taste.

Ladle into four serving bowls, drizzle with the extra coconut milk and dress with the chilli and coriander leaves. **Serves 4**

Hot & sour soup with prawns

Super clean and sinus-clearing, clear tom yum-style broths are nothing like those gelatinous soups that you sometimes get in Chinese restaurants where they've used too much cornflour. They should be hot, vinegary and laden with any vegetables you have in the fridge. I've used a French trick of pouring the broth over shredded lettuce in the bottom of each bowl, so that you get a lovely fresh green contrast to the juicy pink prawns.

1 tablespoon light-flavoured oil
3 tablespoons red curry paste
750ml chicken stock
2 kaffir lime leaves
    or 2 strips lime peel
1 tablespoon sliced ginger
500g green prawns,
    peeled and de-veined
2 small vine-ripened tomatoes
    (about 200g), cut into wedges
3 tablespoons lime juice
2 tablespoons fish sauce
½ head iceberg lettuce, torn into 4 chunks

Heat the oil in a large saucepan over medium heat. Add the curry paste and cook, stirring, for 1–2 minutes or until fragrant. Add the stock, 750ml water, kaffir lime and ginger. Increase the heat to high and bring to the boil, then reduce the heat to very low. Add the prawns and tomatoes and cook for 2–3 minutes.

Season the soup with lime juice and fish sauce. Divide the lettuce between four serving bowls. Ladle the hot soup over the top and serve. **Serves 4**

Miso soup with salmon & coriander

I'm usually quite a purist when it comes to food but there's a hole-in-the-wall Japanese restaurant in London called Dinings which I love that comes up with some great, unconventional flavour combinations that always seem to work. This satisfying soup was inspired by something similar I had there.

3 tablespoons white or red miso paste
1–2 teaspoons chilli paste
800ml dashi, vegetable stock or water
1 tablespoon soy sauce
150g mangetout, shredded
200g salmon, skinned,
    bones removed and diced
handful coriander leaves
2 spring onions, sliced on the diagonal

Put the miso and chilli paste in a large saucepan with the dashi and whisk together. Simmer gently over medium–low heat for 3–4 minutes. Add the soy sauce and simmer for a further minute.

Divide the mangetout and salmon between four serving bowls. Ladle the hot soup into the bowls and top with the coriander leaves and spring onion. **Serves 4**

Salads

My first taste of a Thai beef salad was a shock to the senses, in the best way possible. It was as if I was tasting real flavours for the first time; raw, hot, fresh and alive. And I still love those zingy Thai and Vietnamese combinations but I've also come to appreciate the more subtle salads that the Japanese do so well. Let's face it, any salad is good with me. I'm a strong believer in including some crunch with every meal. Working in Japan turned me on to the idea of having a little salad with breakfast – usually shredded cabbage, seaweed and cherry tomatoes, which I do my own version of using cucumber and avocado with the tomato. But I'm still easing myself into natto (fermented soya bean) and the strange mashed potato dish they serve at breakfast buffets. As well as loving all the opposing flavours in an Asian salad, I'm a texture nut and mouthfeel is such a big element of food from this part of the world. Along with the crisp, raw ingredients I love the contrast of melting salmon, springy squid, soft sweet lychee or crisp wontons. With all these salads, which are designed to be served as main courses – though you can, of course, serve them with anything else you like – it's the dressings that really make them. The perfect balance between sweet, sour, salty and spicy, I can bet you'll become as addicted to them as I am.

MEE REBUS
MEE SIAM
MEE SOTO
NASI LEMAK
LONTONG
RICE

Seared squid salad with lime & coriander

At the end of the eighties grilled octopus with sweet chilli dressing was the dish to order at Paul Merrony's ultra-hip Sydney restaurant Paddington Inn (he also went on to open the Giaconda Dining Room in London). There's nothing quite like that toasty, savoury smell of squid when it's lightly seared – just remember not to toss the squid around too much or it can become tough and stewed.

2 tablespoons soy sauce
1 tablespoon caster sugar
2 tablespoons light-flavoured oil
500g cleaned squid,
    scored on inside and cut into strips
1 red onion, thinly sliced
150g mangetout, halved diagonally
150g sugar snap peas, halved diagonally
handful mixed herbs, such as coriander and mint
lime dressing (see recipe below)

Combine the soy sauce, sugar and oil in a bowl and add the squid. Leave to marinate in the fridge for 10 minutes.

Preheat a barbecue or frying pan until hot. Cook the squid, in batches if necessary, for 1–2 minutes on each side or until just cooked (longer for thicker squid).

Place the red onion, mangetout, peas, herbs and squid in a bowl. Pour over the lime dressing and toss to combine. **Serves 4**

Lime dressing
2 garlic cloves
4 coriander roots
1 teaspoon sea salt
1 teaspoon ground white pepper
2 green chillies, finely sliced
1 tablespoon caster sugar
2 tablespoons lime juice
2 tablespoons fish sauce

Place the garlic, coriander roots, salt, pepper, chilli and sugar in a mortar and pestle and pound to form a paste. Add the lime juice and fish sauce and stir to combine. Set aside.

Prawn & mango salad

This is as simple as an Asian salad can get – you almost feel like you're cheating, there's so little work involved. I made a version using crab instead of prawns for a friend's wedding on a boat in Sydney Harbour once so whenever I make it now it brings back happy memories.

1 small butterhead lettuce, torn
750g cooked prawns, peeled and de-veined
1 mango, peeled, stoned and sliced
1 avocado, peeled, stoned and roughly chopped
1 small red onion, finely sliced
large handful coriander leaves
3 tablespoons sweet chilli sauce
2 tablespoons lime juice
1 tablespoon sesame oil

Arrange the lettuce, prawns, mango, avocado, red onion and coriander leaves on a plate. Whisk together the sweet chilli sauce, lime juice and sesame oil and dress the salad. **Serves 4**

I love the Japanese
tradition of serving
a small salad with
breakfast. If I had
my way I'd have a
bit of crunch with
every meal.

Vietnamese chicken salad with carrot & mint

The Vietnamese really do have a way with raw stuff. Thai salads can almost be overpowering at times – when someone's got carried away with the fish sauce or palm sugar – whereas their neighbours have a knack for creating lighter, fresher, clearer flavours. This one could almost be described as the 'Caesar' of the noughties.

1.5kg barbecued (rotisserie) chicken
90g bean sprouts
180g Chinese cabbage, finely shredded
handful mint leaves
handful basil leaves
pickled carrot (see recipe below)
3 tablespoons fish sauce
3 tablespoons lime juice
2 tablespoons soft brown sugar
1 long red chilli, finely chopped
1 teaspoon finely chopped ginger
1 garlic clove, crushed with the flat of a knife
handful chopped roasted peanuts
small handful crispy shallots

Remove the skin and bones from the chicken and shred the meat. Place the chicken, bean sprouts, cabbage, mint and basil leaves and pickled carrot in a serving bowl.

Make the dressing by whisking together the fish sauce, lime juice, sugar, chilli, ginger and garlic. Pour the dressing over the salad and toss to combine with half the peanuts. Sprinkle with the remaining peanuts and the crispy shallots to serve. **Serves 4**

Pickled carrot
1 large carrot, finely julienned
½ teaspoon sea salt
1½ tablespoons rice vinegar
3 teaspoons caster sugar

Combine all the ingredients in a bowl, cover and leave to pickle for 20 minutes.

Crisp salmon, lychee, coriander & chilli salad

I love the way the salmon in this salad becomes crisp and caramelised on the outside while it's fall-apart soft inside. The oily richness of the fish holds up well to pretty much all Asian flavours and if you're not a fan of lychees (I actually have a weakness for the syrupy-sweet tinned type), you can always use pink grapefruit segments instead.

4 tablespoons fish sauce
3 teaspoons caster sugar
4 skinless salmon fillets (about 180g each)
2 tablespoons light-flavoured oil
300g mangetout
1 small cucumber, finely sliced
20 lychees, peeled, stoned and torn in half,
    or 565g tin, drained
handful coriander leaves
handful basil leaves
2 red chillies, de-seeded and julienned
½ red onion, thinly sliced
2 tablespoons lime juice
2 tablespoons fish sauce

Prepare a marinade for the salmon by combining the fish sauce and 2 teaspoons of the sugar. Place the salmon in the marinade and refrigerate for 10 minutes.

Heat the oil in a large frying pan over medium–high heat and cook the salmon for 1 minute on each of the four sides. Set aside to rest.

Blanch the mangetout in boiling water for 30 seconds, drain and refresh under cold water. Combine with the cucumber, lychees, coriander, basil, chilli and onion in a serving bowl. Break up the salmon and scatter over the top.

Mix together the lime juice, fish sauce and the remaining sugar. Pour over the salad and toss gently to serve. **Serves 4**

Beef salad with orange dressing

The rare beef salad, in all its guises, has become one of the most popular low-carb dishes for Asian food lovers. The sweetly satisfying orange dressing makes a change from the ubiquitous Thai classic and can also be used as a tangy sauce for cold roast beef.

2 tablespoons oyster sauce
1 tablespoon fish sauce
1 tablespoon soft brown sugar
1 teaspoon sesame oil
2 sirloin steaks (about 220g each)
250g asparagus spears, trimmed
150g sugar snap peas
handful mixed herbs,
    such as coriander and basil
1 small red onion, thinly sliced
1 small orange, peeled and thinly sliced
orange dressing (see recipe below)

Put the oyster sauce, fish sauce, sugar and sesame oil in a bowl and stir until the sugar is dissolved. Add the steaks and turn to coat. Cover with cling film and leave to marinate for 1 hour.

Preheat a lightly oiled frying pan over medium–high heat until hot. Sear the steaks to your liking, 2 minutes on either side for rare or 3–4 minutes each side for medium-rare. Transfer to a warm plate and rest for 5 minutes.

Blanch the asparagus and sugar snap peas in a pan of boiling water for a minute or until bright green and tender but still crisp. Rinse under cold running water and drain well. Lightly toss with the herbs, onion and orange. Slice the beef and serve with the asparagus salad and the orange dressing. **Serves 4**

Orange dressing
3 tablespoons orange juice
3 tablespoons extra-virgin olive oil
3 teaspoons red wine vinegar
1 teaspoon soy sauce
1 teaspoon sesame oil
1 teaspoon finely chopped ginger
½ teaspoon caster sugar

Whisk all the ingredients together to combine. Set aside.

Two Japanese salads

I have a very glamorous friend in London who never cooks. She'll get takeaway sushi when we go over for dinner, crack open some champagne and we always have a great night. These salads are for her as they need virtually zero preparation. The dressings can be swapped and served on both salads.

Ohitashi

225g spinach leaves
    (about 2 bunches), trimmed
2 tablespoons soy sauce
1½ tablespoons mirin
bonito flakes (optional)

Bring a medium-sized saucepan of water to the boil. Add the spinach and cook for 1 minute. Drain and refresh under cold water and squeeze to remove all water. Chop and place in a serving bowl. Whisk the soy sauce and mirin together. Drizzle over the spinach and top with bonito flakes if using. **Serves 2**

Tofu salad with a sesame dressing

400g silken tofu,
    drained and cut into cubes
2 tablespoons toasted sesame seeds
    or 1 tablespoon tahini
1 tablespoon caster sugar
1 tablespoon mirin
1 tablespoon soy sauce
4 spring onions, finely chopped

Place the tofu in a serving bowl. Pound the sesame seeds to a paste in a mortar and pestle. Add the sugar, mirin and soy sauce and stir to combine. Drizzle the dressing over the tofu and top with the spring onion. **Serves 2**

Char-grilled chicken salad with pineapple & basil

Pineapple and basil in the same dish is Vietnamese for crazy. It sounds like the most bizarre combination but it's one of those things that just works. The addition of a roughly chopped cashew relish adds an Indonesian satay edge to this dish. Perfect for a summer barbecue.

3 garlic cloves, crushed with
   the flat of a knife
1 tablespoon light brown sugar
3 tablespoons light-flavoured oil
2 tablespoons fish sauce
2 tablespoons lime juice
1 teaspoon turmeric
800g chicken thigh fillets
1 iceberg lettuce, torn
handful basil leaves
1 small pineapple (about 1kg),
   skin removed, cut into long wedges
cashew relish (see recipe below)

Whisk the garlic, brown sugar, 2 tablespoons of the oil, fish sauce, lime juice, turmeric and freshly ground black pepper in a bowl. Add the chicken and leave to marinate in the fridge for 15 minutes.

Heat the char-grill or griddle pan to medium–high. Drizzle with the remaining oil and cook the chicken for 5–6 minutes on each side or until cooked through. Arrange the lettuce, basil leaves and pineapple wedges on a platter, top with the sliced chicken and serve the cashew relish on the side. **Serves 4**

Cashew relish
1 large cucumber, peeled, de-seeded
   and diced
1 red chilli, finely sliced
1 tablespoon fish sauce
1 teaspoon caster sugar
3 tablespoons lime juice
100g roasted cashews, chopped

Place the cucumber, chilli, fish sauce, caster sugar, lime juice and cashews in a bowl and stir to combine. Set aside.

Slaw works with
just about every Asian
dish. Choose red or
white cabbage as
the base and build
from there.

Asian slaw

*I'm a coleslaw freak. Give
me any vegetables grated or
shredded with a drizzle of
dressing and I'm happy – even
more so if the flavours are Asian.
The perfect accompaniment to
grilled or roast meat or fish, the
peanut dressing adds a lovely
rich, nutty edge.*

1 red onion, halved and thinly sliced
500g cabbage, thinly sliced
200g red cabbage, thinly sliced
2 yellow peppers, de-seeded
    and thinly sliced
handful mint leaves
3 tablespoons red wine vinegar
3 tablespoons lemon juice
100ml extra-virgin olive oil
1 tablespoon sesame oil
4 tablespoons soy sauce
3 tablespoons soft brown sugar
1 tablespoon grated ginger
2 garlic cloves, crushed with
    the flat of a knife
4 tablespoons smooth peanut butter

Place the red onion, both cabbages, yellow pepper and mint in
a large bowl. In a separate bowl, whisk together the vinegar,
lemon juice, the oils, soy sauce, sugar, ginger, garlic and peanut
butter. Pour over the vegetables and toss to combine. **Serves 4–6**

Jasmine rice salad

*A throwback to the cold rice
dishes that I remember from
my childhood in the Melbourne
suburbs, this is the perfect
partner to a summer buffet or
barbecue. It can be assembled
very quickly so it's great for
vegetarian emergencies too.*

925g cooked jasmine rice
1 red chilli, de-seeded and julienned
8 spring onions, finely sliced
250g cooked peas
250g cooked sweetcorn
4 tablespoons lime juice
4 tablespoons fish sauce
2 teaspoons sesame oil
1 tablespoon extra-virgin olive oil
1 tablespoon caster sugar

Combine the rice, chilli, spring onion, peas and corn in a large
bowl. In a separate bowl, mix together the lime juice, fish sauce,
the oils and sugar. Pour over the rice and toss to combine.
Season with freshly ground black pepper to taste. **Serves 4–6**

Pork larb with toasted rice

I always ordered this wonderful dish at a place called Thai Isan (named after the north-eastern region of Thailand) on Bondi Road in Sydney. I remember going there with a vegan friend who was so fussy she wouldn't even eat certain vegetables like aubergine or mushrooms, but she could drink more red wine than anyone else I knew.

1 tablespoon jasmine rice
1 garlic clove, chopped
1 tablespoon finely chopped lemon grass
1 green chilli, chopped
2 tablespoons light-flavoured oil
500g pork or chicken mince
3 spring onions, finely sliced
2 teaspoons caster sugar
2 tablespoons fish sauce
4 tablespoons lime juice
1 teaspoon dried chilli flakes
1 kaffir lime leaf, thinly sliced
4 thin wedges green cabbage
120g snake beans or green beans,
    cut into 15cm lengths
large handful coriander leaves

Toast the rice in a small dry frying pan over medium–low heat for about 10 minutes, stirring regularly, until lightly toasted. Use a mortar and pestle to pound the toasted rice until finely crushed. Remove and set aside, then pound the garlic, lemon grass and chilli into a paste.

Heat a wok over high heat. Add the oil and, when hot, add the mince and spring onion. Cook for 3–4 minutes or until browned. Remove the wok from the heat. Add the garlic and chilli paste, sugar, fish sauce, lime juice, chilli flakes and kaffir lime and stir to combine.

To serve, place the mince on a platter with the cabbage wedges and dress with the beans, coriander leaves and crushed rice.
Serves 4

Seafood

Coming from a family of butchers where for a long time the only fish we ate was in fingers or served with chips, I was drawn to real seafood later in life. Now I love how we're all more educated about our fish these days, and Asian food is the perfect excuse for us to get acquainted with the local fishmonger. It's easy to forget there are seasons when certain types of fish are available, just like there are for fruit and vegetables. Fish and shellfish are the perfect partners to Asian flavours; the two complement each other so well, creating light, clean and healthy dishes. Cooking with them always transports me to the incredible, glistening fish market in Tokyo and the shores of Southeast Asia. Though I do have a not-so-happy memory from one of my first visits to Thailand when, quite late at night, my friend and I came across what we thought was a great little place to stay in Koh Phangan. We couldn't work out why it was so cheap, until we woke up the next morning to the pungent smell of the fish-drying yard right outside our window! I still can't bear the smell of shrimp paste.

These days, whenever
I'm cooking fish, I find
I increasingly prefer
using Asian ingredients
over any other. There's
something about the
clean, fresh taste and
soft texture of seafood
that copes so well
with the onslaught of
ginger, garlic, chilli
and soy combinations –
not forgetting a squeeze
of lime.

Fish with lime butter two ways

This is a bit of a no-cook recipe, really. It's a great example of how using butter instead of the usual oils associated with Asian cooking can lift the flavours in a completely different, slightly more indulgent, way. I also like to vary it by adding chilli, coriander or ginger, depending on my mood.

Pan-fried fish with bok choy & lime butter
4 thick white fish fillets (about 800g)
1 tablespoon light-flavoured oil
2 heads bok choy, halved
lime butter (see recipe below)

Season the fish with sea salt and freshly ground black pepper. Heat the oil in a large non-stick frying pan over medium–high heat until hot. Add the fish and cook for 2 minutes on each side or until the fish is cooked, turning just once.

Blanch the bok choy in a large pan of lightly salted boiling water for 2–3 minutes until bright green and tender. Drain well. Serve dressed with the lime butter on top of the fish. **Serves 4**

Fish baked in a bag with lime butter & potatoes
1 small potato (I like to use 'Desirée)
4 white fish fillets (about 180g each)
lime butter (see recipe below)
handful coriander leaves

Preheat the oven to 200°C/gas mark 6. Bring a small saucepan of salted water to the boil. Peel the potato and slice very thinly with a mandolin. Blanch in the boiling water for 2 minutes or until just tender. Remove from the water with a slotted spoon and drain well.

Take a 30cm square piece of non-stick baking paper and arrange a quarter of the potato in a single layer in the centre. Place one fish fillet on the sliced potato, season with sea salt and freshly ground black pepper, and top with the lime butter. Join the two horizontal sides of the paper and fold twice to seal the top of the parcel. Fold the two vertical sides underneath the parcel. Repeat with the remaining potato and fish.

Place the parcels on a baking tray and cook on one of the lower shelves in the oven for 14–16 minutes, depending on the thickness of the fish, until just cooked through. Serve the fish parcels on individual plates. Open the top of the baking paper bag and dress with coriander leaves. **Serves 4**

Lime butter
50g unsalted butter, softened
grated zest ½ lime
1 tablespoon lime juice
½ teaspoon sea salt

In a mixing bowl, whisk together all the ingredients. Not all the lime juice will mix in with the butter, this is fine.

Barbecued prawns with three dipping sauces

I may be opening myself up for 'throw another prawn on the barbie' jokes here, but without wanting to be too much of an Australian cliché, this is a foolproof party dish that requires almost zero effort. What's not to love?

1.25kg large raw prawns, heads and veins removed, leaving shells intact
2 tablespoons light-flavoured oil

Toss the prawns and oil in a large bowl to coat. Preheat a barbecue to hot with the lid down. Cook for 2–3 minutes on each side. Serve the prawns with the dipping sauces. **Serves 4**

Soy, chilli & garlic dipping sauce

2 red chillies, de-seeded and chopped
3 garlic cloves, chopped
1 teaspoon granulated sugar
2 tablespoons light-flavoured oil
3 tablespoons soy sauce
1 tablespoon chopped coriander leaves
1–2 tablespoons chopped spring onions

Place the chilli, garlic and sugar in a mortar and pestle and pound to a paste. Heat the oil in a small saucepan. Pour the hot oil over the chilli mix and stir. Add the soy sauce. Leave to cool. Add the coriander and spring onion and serve with the prawns.

Green chilli mayonnaise

1 garlic clove
½ teaspoon sea salt
2 long green chillies, de-seeded and chopped
250g good-quality mayonnaise (or use recipe below)
1 spring onion, finely sliced

Use a mortar and pestle to pound the garlic, salt and chilli to a paste. Stir in the mayonnaise and season with salt and freshly ground black pepper to taste. Garnish with the spring onion.

Mayonnaise

2 egg yolks
1 tablespoon lime juice
250ml light-flavoured oil

Use a blender to blend the egg yolks and lime juice until well combined. With the motor running, slowly add the oil, 1 tablespoon at a time, until thick and creamy.

Chilli fish sauce

6 small red chillies, finely chopped
2 tablespoons fish sauce
¼ lime

Combine the chilli and fish sauce. Squeeze in the lime juice and any pulp from the lime and mix well.

Tuna kebabs with crispy coleslaw

The Japanese take their yakitori (chicken on skewers) and kushiyaki (everything and anything on skewers) very seriously, even down to the 'binchotan' or white charcoal that it's grilled over. A regular grill will do for this tasty seven-minute supper.

2 tablespoons soy sauce
1 tablespoon mirin
2 tuna steaks, cubed
1 teaspoon wasabi paste
125ml good-quality mayonnaise
4 spring onions, cut into 6cm lengths
crispy coleslaw (see recipe below)
2 lemons, cut into wedges

Soak 8 wooden skewers in water for 1 hour to prevent them scorching. Mix the soy sauce and mirin together in a bowl. Add the tuna and set aside to marinate for 1 hour in the fridge. Meanwhile, whisk together the wasabi paste and mayonnaise, adding a dash of hot water to thin. Set aside.

Thread the tuna and spring onions alternately onto the skewers and barbecue or fry in a lightly oiled pan over high heat for 1 minute on each side. Serve with the wasabi mayonnaise, crispy coleslaw and lemon wedges. **Serves 4**

Crispy coleslaw
1 teaspoon sesame oil
2 tablespoons soy sauce
2 teaspoons caster sugar
1 tablespoon lime juice
½ red chilli, de-seeded and finely chopped
500g Chinese cabbage, shredded
200g mangetout, thinly sliced on the diagonal
2 celery sticks cut into thin 5cm-long batons
3 spring onions, finely sliced on the diagonal
1 tablespoon sesame seeds, roasted

To make the dressing, place the sesame oil, soy sauce, sugar, lime juice and chilli in a bowl and whisk to combine.

Place the shredded cabbage, mangetout, celery, spring onion and dressing in a large bowl and toss to combine. Dress with the sesame seeds to serve.

Red fish curry

This is one of those recipes I almost feel guilty for including as it's so quick and easy and, apart from the fish, can be made with store cupboard ingredients. Tasty, healthy and so simple, it's one of my favourite 20 minute dinners. Adding lime juice and fresh basil towards the end really lifts the dish.

1 tablespoon light-flavoured oil
3 tablespoons red curry paste
400g tin diced tomatoes
1 tablespoon soft brown sugar
500g butternut squash,
    cut into 3–4cm pieces
500g skinless firm white fish fillets,
    cut into 3cm pieces
250g snake beans or green beans,
    cut into 5cm lengths
3 tablespoons fish sauce
1 tablespoon lime juice
handful basil leaves

Heat the oil in a medium-sized saucepan over medium heat. Add the curry paste and cook for 1–2 minutes or until fragrant. Add the tomatoes, 500ml water, sugar and butternut squash. Reduce the heat and simmer for 15 minutes or until the squash is nearly tender. Add the fish and snake beans and simmer for another 2–3 minutes or until just cooked. Add the fish sauce, lime juice and basil leaves. Serve with steamed rice. **Serves 4**

Salt & pepper whiting

Who really wants to start messing about with batter in the kitchen? If you marinate these little fish (or you can use fish pieces) in fish sauce then toss them in the seasoned flour and shallow-fry, they become beautifully crisp and golden. As well as the grapefruit salad you could also serve them with the green chilli mayo on page 86.

75g plain flour
2 teaspoons dried chilli flakes
2 teaspoons freshly ground black pepper
600g skinless small white fish fillets
    or sliced larger white fish fillets
3 tablespoons fish sauce
light-flavoured oil, for deep-frying
grapefruit salad (see recipe below)
2 limes, cut into wedges

Combine the flour, chilli flakes and pepper in a bowl. Marinate the fish fillets in the fish sauce for 5 minutes, then drain one by one and roll in the spiced flour. Heat the oil in a deep frying pan over medium–high heat until hot. Fry the fish in batches for 2 minutes or until golden. Remove from the pan with a slotted spoon, drain well and place on kitchen paper to drain completely. Serve with the grapefruit salad and lime wedges. **Serves 4**

Grapefruit salad
2 red grapefruit, cut into segments
large handful mint leaves
large handful coriander leaves
1 small red onion, cut into thin wedges
2 teaspoons fish sauce
1 tablespoon caster sugar
2 tablespoons lime juice

Combine the grapefruit, mint, coriander and onion in a bowl. Whisk the fish sauce, sugar and lime juice together in another bowl and pour over the salad.

Stir-fried prawns with chilli & tomato

When I first had kids I was one of those terrible, righteous, try-hard parents who didn't allow their kids to have ketchup or sugar. I've come to realise that a bit of tomato sauce from a bottle won't kill you – but I still prefer if it's organic! This was my father's favourite at our local Chinese restaurant so I always think of him when I make it.

1kg large prawns, peeled
    and de-veined, tails intact
2 tablespoons cornflour
2 teaspoons sesame oil
5 tablespoons light-flavoured oil
1 large red onion, cut into wedges
2 yellow peppers, cut into strips
3 red chillies, de-seeded and quartered
3cm piece ginger, peeled and julienned
4 garlic cloves, crushed with
    the flat of a knife
3 tablespoons mirin or white wine
4 tablespoons soy sauce
2 tablespoons granulated sugar
2 teaspoons sesame oil, extra
3 tablespoons tomato ketchup

Place the prawns in a large bowl, dust with the cornflour and drizzle with the sesame oil. Stir to coat and set aside for 10 minutes. Heat 3 tablespoons of the oil in a wok or large frying pan over high heat. Add the prawns and cook, tossing often, for 1–2 minutes, until nearly cooked through. Remove from the wok.

Reduce heat to medium and add the remaining 2 tablespoons of oil. Add the onion, yellow pepper, chilli, ginger and garlic and stir-fry for 2 minutes. Whisk together the mirin, soy sauce, sugar, extra sesame oil and tomato ketchup in a bowl until the sugar dissolves. Add to the wok, along with the prawns, and stir-fry for 1–2 minutes. Serve immediately. **Serves 4**

Glazed salmon with cucumber sesame salad

Salmon has a reputation for being the chicken breast of the fish world, and there's nothing wrong with that. Regarded as the healthy option, it's also packed with flavour, stands up to Asian ingredients and marinades beautifully. If you're bored with teriyaki, this is the recipe for you.

4 tablespoons mirin
4 tablespoons soy sauce
2 tablespoons soft brown sugar
1 tablespoon lemon juice
4 skinless salmon fillets (about 175g each)
cucumber sesame salad (see recipe below)

Stir the mirin, soy sauce, sugar and lemon juice together in a bowl until combined. Put the salmon fillets in a shallow dish, pour the mixture over them and set aside in the fridge to marinate for 5–10 minutes.

Preheat the grill to high and line a grill tray with foil. Remove the salmon from the marinade, setting the marinade aside, and place the salmon on the tray. Grill for about 7 minutes or until the fish is nicely coloured and still pink in the centre.

Meanwhile, pour the salmon marinade into a small frying pan and cook over high heat for 3–4 minutes, until reduced to a glaze. Pour over the cooked salmon. Serve the glazed salmon with the cucumber sesame salad. **Serves 4**

Cucumber sesame salad
1 tablespoon mirin
1 tablespoon rice vinegar
1 teaspoon sesame oil
2 small cucumbers

Whisk together the mirin, vinegar and sesame oil. Use a vegetable peeler or mandolin to peel long ribbons from the cucumber. Toss the cucumber ribbons with the dressing.

Fish and shellfish are
the perfect partners
to Asian flavours;
the two complement
each other so well,
creating light, clean
and healthy dishes.

Fish sambal

Sambal is a classic Southeast Asian relish, usually made with dried shrimp. I do my version with anchovies, which I tend to have in my store cupboard. Leftover sambal is delicious with anything barbecued.

6 red chillies, de-seeded and chopped
1 red onion, roughly chopped
3 tinned anchovies
1 teaspoon sea salt
1 lemon grass stalk,
    white part only, chopped
5 tablespoons light-flavoured oil
1 teaspoon granulated sugar
4 skinless white fish fillets,
    such as snapper (about 175g each)
1 small head cos lettuce, leaves separated
coconut rice (see page 199)

Place the chilli, onion, anchovies, sea salt, lemon grass and 4 tablespoons of the oil in a food processor and pulse until smooth. Heat a large frying pan over low heat, add the sambal and fry gently, stirring regularly, for 10 minutes, to lose any raw flavour. Add the sugar and leave to cool.

Heat the remaining tablespoon of oil in a large frying pan over medium–high heat. Season the fish with sea salt and freshly ground black pepper and fry until just cooked through. Serve with the cos lettuce, coconut rice and the sambal. **Serves 4**

Baked fish with sticky sauce

There are some people who are terrified by the idea of serving a whole fish but it really couldn't be easier. The trick is knowing how to serve it: you just cut down the middle, open it up with a knife and fork and lift out the backbone. And the taste is worth any tiny bones that are left behind.

1kg fish, such as snapper or sea bass,
    side fins trimmed
1 lemon, sliced
2 tablespoons light-flavoured oil
3 garlic cloves, sliced
3cm piece ginger, peeled and julienned
3 red chillies, thinly sliced
2 tablespoons light brown sugar
4 tablespoons fish sauce
100ml lime juice (about 5 limes)
2 spring onions, sliced
small handful mixed herbs,
    such as basil and coriander

Preheat the oven to 190°C/gas mark 5 and brush a baking tray with oil. Make three deep slashes on either side of the fish, insert the lemon slices in the slashes and place on the tray and bake for 25 minutes.

Meanwhile, heat 1 tablespoon of the oil in a wok over high heat. Add the garlic, ginger and chilli and stir-fry for 1–2 minutes. Add the sugar, fish sauce and lime juice and cook for 5–6 minutes or until syrupy. Pour into a jug and set aside.

Serve the fish on a platter. Drizzle over the sauce and dress with the spring onion and mixed herbs. **Serves 4**

Turmeric fish

Although I've never actually been to Vietnam I've been to plenty of Vietnamese restaurants in Sydney and London, and I love them. So this is my take on Hanoi fish, a classic I've eaten so many times I feel like I've been to the place it originated!

4 tablespoons light-flavoured oil
1 teaspoon turmeric
½ teaspoon caster sugar
½ teaspoon sea salt
4 firm white fish fillets,
    such as snapper (about 150g each)
coriander leaves, roughly chopped
1 lemon, cut into wedges

Whisk together half the oil, the turmeric, sugar and sea salt in a shallow dish. Add the fish, toss to coat and set aside in the fridge to marinate for 5 minutes.

Heat the remaining oil in a large non-stick frying pan over medium–high heat. Add the fish and cook, turning once, for 5–6 minutes or until cooked through. Remove from the pan. Dress with the coriander and lemon wedges and serve with steamed Asian greens and steamed rice. **Serves 4**

Poultry

I'm sure you don't need me telling you that, just as it is for many other cultures, chicken is the most traditional canvas used in Asian cooking. As well as it being reasonably cheap and easy to find, the lean white meat is the perfect partner for the delicately spicy, fragrant flavours, which you can play down or oomph up as you choose. Chicken is the second most searched recipe item on the internet (after pasta) and always the most popular choice in Asian restaurants – I can never look at lemon chicken in a Chinese restaurant without thinking of my grandmother. And you only have to see all the glossy red roast ducks hanging in the window of any barbecue shop in Chinatown to understand how popular their web-footed cousins are too. A lot of people fear eating undercooked chicken but overcooking can result in something so tough you can hardly cut through. There's nothing wrong with the chicken being moist, juicy and even faintly pink at the centre – something I learnt in Japan, where they serve chicken sashimi! The other good thing about using chicken in Asian cooking is that you don't have to worry about finding the finest bird money can buy – a basic chook, and often just the meatier thighs and drumsticks are all you need to create an irresistible dish.

Pan-fried duck breast with plum sauce

Asian cultures have a way with duck, pairing the rich, dark meat with sweet, fruity flavours. The duck holds strong, aromatic notes so well but it's always good, as with everyone's favourite crispy duck, to serve it with a cucumber salad or something else clean-tasting to cut through the richness.

4 duck breasts (about 175g each), with skin
½ teaspoon sea salt
½ teaspoon freshly ground black pepper
½ teaspoon Chinese five spice powder
1 teaspoon julienned ginger
8 plums, halved and stoned
2 tablespoons honey
2 tablespoons soy sauce
1 cinnamon stick
2 star anise
1 tablespoon lime juice

Score the skin of the duck breasts and season with the salt, pepper and five spice powder. Place the breasts in a large frying pan, skin side down, and cook over high heat for 1 minute, then reduce the heat to low and cook for 8 minutes to render the fat. Turn the duck over and cook for 6 minutes. Remove from the pan and transfer to a warm plate, cover with foil and set aside to rest.

Pour off the excess duck fat and fry the ginger for 2 minutes. Add the plums to the pan then add the honey, soy sauce, cinnamon stick, star anise and lime juice. Cook for 5 minutes, stirring occasionally, until juicy and softened.

Slice the duck breasts and serve with the sauce. Accompany with steamed rice and greens or a simple cucumber salad. **Serves 4**

Chicken & mushroom croquettes with baby cos

Croquettes, rissoles, call them what you will, these little bite-size morsels have a certain retro appeal that makes them perfect with drinks if you're having friends over. As they're made with chicken they'll colour better if you pan-fry them, but you can pop them in the oven if you're pushed for time.

4 tablespoons light-flavoured oil
250g button mushrooms,
    stalks removed and finely chopped
2 garlic cloves, crushed with
    the flat of a knife
500g chicken mince
1 teaspoon finely chopped ginger
1 tablespoon light soy sauce
1 teaspoon sesame oil
½ teaspoon freshly cracked black pepper
1 or 2 heads baby cos, leaves separated
1 small red onion, cut into rings
small handful coriander leaves

Heat a large frying pan over medium–low heat. Add 1 tablespoon of the oil and cook the mushrooms and garlic for about 5 minutes or until nearly all the moisture has evaporated. Remove the mushrooms from the pan and cool.

Combine the chicken mince with the ginger, soy sauce, sesame oil and pepper. Add the mushrooms and mix well. Use 2 tablespoons of the mixture at a time to form into croquettes.

Heat the remaining oil in a frying pan over medium–high heat. Add the croquettes in two batches and cook, turning occasionally, for 5–7 minutes or until golden all over and cooked through. Serve immediately with the lettuce leaves, onion rings and coriander. **Serves 4**

Hoisin chicken with a celery salad

This classic dish has an almost fifties feel to it, it's been around for so long. It's a great standby if you have hungry kids to feed – they love getting their fingers and faces sticky eating the thighs. A jar of rich, dark, tangy hoisin sauce kept in the fridge can also be used to liven up endless other dishes.

100ml hoisin sauce
1 tablespoon Chinese chilli sauce
2 teaspoons grated ginger
3 garlic cloves, crushed with the
    flat of a knife
2 tablespoons soy sauce
2 tablespoons lemon juice
½ teaspoon Chinese five spice powder
8 skinless chicken thighs (about 1kg)
celery salad (see recipe below)
1 tablespoon sesame seeds

Preheat the oven to 200°C/gas mark 6. Line a baking tray with foil. Mix the hoisin and chilli sauces, ginger, garlic, soy sauce, lemon juice and five spice powder in a large bowl. Add the chicken and leave to marinate in the fridge for 15 minutes.

Arrange the chicken on the prepared tray and bake for 30–35 minutes. Serve with the celery salad and a sprinkling of sesame seeds. **Serves 4**

Celery salad
200g green beans,
    cut into 5cm lengths
2 teaspoons soy sauce
¼ teaspoon sesame oil
2 teaspoons rice vinegar
2 teaspoons honey
2 celery sticks,
    finely sliced into 5cm batons

Blanch the beans in a pan of lightly salted boiling water for 2–3 minutes until they are bright green and tender yet crisp. Rinse under cold running water and drain well. Combine the soy sauce, sesame oil, vinegar and honey to make a dressing. Drizzle over the celery and beans.

Green curry has become such a popular dish I can't help wondering whether it's eaten more by people in other countries than it ever has been in Thailand.

Thai green chicken curry

I really wrestled with the decision over whether or not the world needed another green curry recipe, and I'm still not sure it does! But this is one of the few recipes in the book for which I've made the paste from scratch. It's so worth it and, if you make plenty, you can keep it the fridge as an emergency marinade or seasoning for virtually anything.

1 tablespoon light-flavoured oil
3 tablespoons green curry paste
  (see recipe below)
125ml chicken stock or water
250ml coconut milk
1 anchovy, finely chopped
4 kaffir lime leaves, torn
  or 3 strips lime peel
500g chicken breast fillets, cut into chunks
100g snake beans or green beans, cut into batons
handful fresh or tinned baby corn
400g aubergines, cut into chunks
1 tablespoon granulated sugar
2 tablespoons fish sauce
1 tablespoon lime juice
handful basil leaves
3 green chillies, de-seeded and sliced

Heat a large saucepan over high heat. Add the oil and cook the curry paste for 2 minutes or until fragrant.

Add the stock, coconut milk, anchovy and kaffir lime and cook over medium–low heat for 5 minutes. Add the chicken and cook for 5 minutes.

Add the snake beans, corn, aubergine, sugar, fish sauce and lime juice and cook for 4–5 minutes. Scatter with the basil leaves and chilli and serve with steamed rice. **Serves 4**

Green curry paste
1 teaspoon white peppercorns
1 teaspoon coriander seeds
½ teaspoon cumin seeds
1 teaspoon sea salt
1 teaspoon turmeric
1 lemon grass stalk, chopped
6 garlic cloves, chopped
4 shallots or 1 small red onion, chopped
2 tablespoons coriander roots
  or stems, chopped
3cm piece ginger, peeled and chopped
4 green chillies, de-seeded and chopped
2 tablespoons light-flavoured oil

Heat a small saucepan over medium heat. Add the peppercorns, coriander and cumin seeds and toast the spices for 1–2 minutes or until fragrant. Place the toasted spices, salt, turmeric, lemon grass, garlic, shallots, coriander, ginger, chilli and oil in a food processor and pulse to a paste. **Makes about 250g**

Classic stir-fried chicken with basil

This is the sort of stir-fry you might make for your first ever dinner party, it's so easy to prepare and always a crowd pleaser. I'm not sure I've ever used the real Thai or holy basil as the proper stuff's called, as I tend to throw in regular Italian basil and it works a treat. And I kind of like the fusion factor, and throwing caution to the wind!

4 garlic cloves
2 large red chillies
¼ teaspoon sea salt
2 tablespoons light-flavoured oil
600g chicken mince
400g snake beans or green beans,
    cut into 5cm lengths on the diagonal
2 tablespoons fish sauce
1 tablespoon dark soy sauce
1 tablespoon caster sugar
small handful Asian basil leaves
    or regular basil
pinch ground white pepper

Pound the garlic, one chilli and salt in a mortar and pestle until it forms a paste. Alternatively, place the garlic and chilli on a chopping board, sprinkle with the salt and finely chop with a knife using the side of the blade to make a paste. Slice the remaining chilli thinly.

Heat a wok or large non-stick frying pan over medium–high heat. Add the oil and the garlic paste and sliced chilli and cook, stirring, for 30 seconds or until the garlic starts to colour. Add the mince and cook, stirring, for about 2 minutes or until starting to brown, then add the beans and cook for a further minute. Add the fish sauce, soy sauce and sugar and stir-fry for a further 30 seconds.

Remove from the heat, stir in the basil leaves and white pepper. Serve immediately with steamed rice. **Serves 4**

Stir-fried Vietnamese lemon grass chicken

It's funny to think that almost every table had a little shaker of white pepper on it, along with the salt, up until the seventies when everyone suddenly started waving black pepper mills around. Nothing beats the very Vietnamese combination of white pepper and lemon however, so it's always worth having both in the kitchen.

3 garlic cloves
1 teaspoon turmeric
2 large green chillies, diced
2 lemon grass stalks, white part only,
    very finely sliced or grated zest 2 lemons
1 teaspoon sea salt
800g skinless chicken thigh fillets,
    cut into chunks
3 tablespoons light-flavoured oil
2 celery sticks, cut into batons
1 bunch asparagus (about 200g),
    trimmed and halved
2 tablespoons fish sauce
1 tablespoon soy sauce
2 tablespoons lemon juice
2 teaspoons granulated sugar
3 spring onions, cut into batons

Pound the garlic, turmeric, chilli, lemon grass and salt in a mortar and pestle until a paste is formed. Combine with the chicken in a bowl and mix well. Cover and set aside to marinate in the fridge for 10 minutes.

Heat a wok or large frying pan over high heat. Add half the oil and half the chicken and stir-fry for 2–3 minutes. Remove from the wok and repeat with the remaining oil and chicken. Return the chicken to the wok, add the celery and asparagus and stir-fry for 2 minutes. Add the fish sauce, soy sauce, lemon juice, sugar, spring onion and freshly ground white pepper and toss over the heat for a further minute. Serve immediately with steamed rice. **Serves 4**

Thai barbecued yellow chicken

If you don't have one of those big barbecues, you can cook this in the oven first and then finish it off outside. And if you don't have an outside area to eat in, let alone a barbecue, you can just bake this for 45 minutes in a 200°C/gas mark 6 oven or until browned and cooked through. Serve with a big, crunchy salad.

3 garlic cloves, crushed with
    the flat of a knife
1 tablespoon granulated sugar
3 tablespoons fish sauce
2 tablespoons lime juice
1 tablespoon light-flavoured oil
1 teaspoon turmeric
1 teaspoon sea salt
1 tablespoon ground coriander
1.5kg chicken, jointed into 8 pieces
1 lemon, cut into wedges

Whisk together the garlic, sugar, fish sauce, lime juice, oil, turmeric, salt and coriander in a large bowl. Add the chicken pieces and toss to coat. Leave to marinate in the fridge for 1 hour.

Preheat a well-oiled barbecue to hot. Reduce the heat to medium–low, add the chicken and cook for 18–20 minutes, turning every few minutes to prevent burning, until the chicken is cooked through. Serve with lemon wedges. **Serves 4**

Cashew & chicken curry

A play on Malaysian and Singaporean flavours, this simple, gentle curry is made creamy with the addition of blended cashew nuts, which impart a lovely sweet flavour without being too rich. It's also inspired by a dish the whole family look forward to having in Singapore – one of our favourite foodie stopovers.

20g butter
1 tablespoon light-flavoured oil
2 red onions, chopped
1 teaspoon sea salt
3 garlic cloves, finely chopped
1 tablespoon julienned ginger
1–2 green chillies, finely chopped
3 tablespoons curry powder
400g tin chopped tomatoes
1.5kg chicken, cut into pieces
    or 1.5kg chicken pieces
2 teaspoons granulated sugar
250ml natural yoghurt
155g roasted cashews, ground
2 teaspoons fish sauce
large handful coriander leaves,
    roughly chopped
flatbread or naan

Heat the butter and oil in a large heavy-based pan over medium heat. Add the onion and salt and cook, stirring, for 5–6 minutes or until soft. Add the garlic, ginger, chilli and curry powder and cook, continuing to stir, for 2 minutes. Add the tomatoes, chicken and sugar and cover the pan. Simmer gently for 25–30 minutes, stirring occasionally.

Add the yoghurt, cashews and fish sauce and cook over low heat for 5 minutes. Do not allow to boil. Remove from the heat, dress with the coriander and serve with the bread. **Serves 4**

Sticky soy roast chicken

This is a great way to jazz up a whole chicken. The soy sauce, brown sugar and red onion glaze gives the bird a lovely glossy sheen and tastes incredible. Served with a big pile of leafy greens, I'll be very surprised if this doesn't become a family favourite.

1.5kg chicken
100ml oyster sauce
4 tablespoons soy sauce
3 tablespoons soft brown sugar
4 garlic cloves, roughly chopped
1 small red onion, chopped
Chinese chilli sauce

Preheat the oven to 200°C/gas mark 6. Rinse the chicken, pat dry and prick deeply all over with a fork. Blend the oyster sauce, soy sauce, sugar, garlic and onion in a food processor until finely chopped. Rub the marinade all over the chicken, inside and out, reserving some marinade for basting.

Put the chicken, breast side up, in a large roasting tray. Roast for 20 minutes then brush with the marinade. Repeat this step. Roast for another 20–30 minutes or until the juices run clear when you prick the thickest part of the thigh (cover the chicken with foil if it's browning too quickly). Let the chicken rest for 10 minutes before carving, Chinese style, into pieces through the bone. Serve with Chinese chilli sauce and steamed rice. **Serves 4**

Spa-style poached chicken with sesame bean salad

There's a trick to poaching chicken that I've been doing ever since I first opened bills. It's ridiculously simple – you just bring the water to the boil then turn off the heat, put the chicken in and cover and leave it to poach for 20 minutes. Don't be put off by the amount of salt I've used for the poaching water, you'll find it gives the chicken a great flavour lift.

3 coriander stems
1 teaspoon black peppercorns
2 spring onions, roughly chopped
1 tablespoon sea salt
4 skinless chicken breast fillets
    (about 200g each)
sesame bean salad (see recipe below)
2 red chillies, finely chopped
steamed brown rice (see page 199)

Put the coriander, peppercorns, spring onion and sea salt in a large saucepan filled with cold water and bring to the boil. Add the chicken, turn off the heat, cover and leave to poach for 20 minutes.

Slice the chicken breasts into serving size pieces. Dress the bean salad and serve with the chicken, chopped chilli and steamed brown rice. **Serves 4**

Sesame bean salad
500g green beans
2 tablespoons soy sauce
2 tablespoons rice vinegar
3 tablespoons mirin
1 tablespoon sesame oil
3 garlic cloves, finely chopped
1 tablespoon finely chopped ginger
1 tablespoon toasted sesame seeds

Blanch the beans in a pan of lightly salted water for 2–3 minutes until they are bright green and tender yet crisp. Rinse under cold running water and drain well.

To make the dressing, in a small saucepan, bring the soy sauce, vinegar, mirin and sesame oil to the boil. Take the pan off the heat and add the garlic, ginger and sesame seeds.

Pork

As we become more knowledgeable about meat – where it's
from, what breed and so on – pork is making something of a
comeback and is becoming quite a delicacy again. When I was
a kid I remember a pork chop with a ring of pineapple on top
– tinned, of course – being the height of sophistication! And I
remember my grandfather telling me that when Vietnamese
butchers began setting up in Australia in the seventies, they
started a trend for 'new fashion pork', showing how a pig could
be butchered in different ways so you could get the lean cuts as
well as the fatty ones. It was good timing as it was just before
everyone began obsessing about aerobics and keeping fit, and
pork loin became the popular low-fat meat of choice. These
days, people appear to be less concerned about their waistlines
as everyone is pork belly crazy, particularly in restaurants, and
I for one find it impossible to resist its rich, melting goodness.
Whether you like it fatty or lean, pork is such a mild and versatile
meat that takes sweet, and sticky flavours as well as salty ones
incredibly well, which makes it ideal for this kind of cooking.

Pork baguettes with meatballs

These always remind me of a wonderful food stylist friend who became addicted to 'banh mi' when she was pregnant and, although we usually ate whatever food we were photographing in the studio, would send her assistant out to get them every day. They make a great al fresco or barbecue dinner in the summer.

600g pork mince
3 garlic cloves, crushed with
   the flat of a knife
1 tablespoon finely grated ginger
½ teaspoon sea salt
¼ teaspoon ground white pepper
1 spring onion, finely chopped
1 green chilli, de-seeded
   and finely chopped
3 tablespoons light-flavoured oil
1 long French baguette
¼ iceberg lettuce, leaves separated
pickled carrot (see recipe page 63)
handful mint leaves
handful coriander leaves
chilli and garlic mayonnaise
   (see recipe below)

Combine the pork, garlic, ginger, salt, pepper, spring onion and green chilli in a bowl. With your hands, roll the mix into bite-size balls, about 2.5cm in diameter. Heat a barbecue grill to high heat and drizzle with the oil. Cook the meatballs for about 2 minutes on each side, flattening them slightly, until cooked through.

Slice the baguette into four sections and serve with the meatballs, lettuce, pickled carrot and herbs and the chilli and garlic mayonnaise. **Serves 4**

Chilli & garlic mayonnaise
100g good-quality mayonnaise
   (shop bought or see page 86)
1 teaspoon Chinese chilli sauce or finely chopped chilli
1 garlic clove, finely grated

Combine all the ingredients, adjusting the chilli to taste.

Vietnamese pork chops

I have fond memories of sneaking away from work to Sydney's Chinatown at lunchtime and having this – it's a bit like a Vietnamese version of a fry-up. It should be served with steamed rice, raw vegetables and even a fried egg, if you like.

1 tablespoon granulated sugar
2 tablespoons fish sauce
4 garlic cloves, crushed with
    the flat of a knife
1 tablespoon light-flavoured oil
4 pork loin steaks (about 220g each)
    or pork chops
nuoc cham (see page 15)

Stir the sugar, fish sauce, garlic and oil together in a shallow dish. With a sharp knife, cut slashes about 2cm apart in the pork rind and then add the pork to the dish and stir well. Cover and allow to marinate in the fridge for 15 minutes.

Heat a large non-stick frying pan over medium heat and cook the pork for 8–10 minutes, turning halfway through. Using tongs, hold the pork with the fat side down, moving the meat around until all the rind is browned.

Serve with steamed rice, an assortment of crisp raw vegetables and nuoc cham. **Serves 4**

Pork with peppercorns

It's funny, now that I live in London I'm actually closer to a store where I can buy fresh green peppercorns than I was in Sydney – that's the foodie revolution for you! It can be tricky to find them fresh, however, and this comes up just as well with the tinned sort. Either way, they cut through the richness of the sauce and give the dish a nice heat.

400g pork shoulder, cut into strips
    or pork stir-fry strips
3 tablespoons green curry paste
    (shop bought or see page 115)
2 tablespoons light-flavoured oil
3 green chillies, de-seeded and chopped
400g green beans, cut into 4cm lengths
    on the diagonal
125ml coconut milk
3–4 tablespoons fish sauce
1 teaspoon granulated sugar
1–2 tablespoons tinned green peppercorns
small handful basil leaves

Combine the pork with the curry paste. Heat 1 tablespoon of the oil in a large wok or frying pan over high heat. Add the pork and stir-fry for 2 minutes or until just cooked. Remove and set aside.

Return the wok to a high heat, add the remaining oil. Add the chilli and green beans and stir-fry for 2 minutes. Add the coconut milk, fish sauce, sugar and peppercorns and stir to combine. Return the pork to the wok and cook for a further minute or until heated through. Scatter over the basil leaves and serve with steamed rice. **Serves 4**

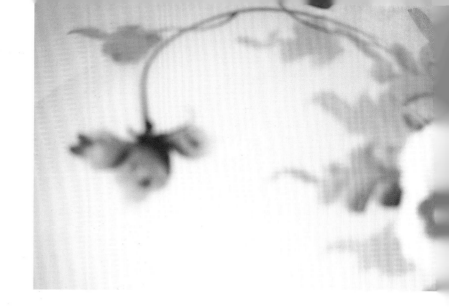

I can be a big fan of food nostalgia, and Japanese curry somehow satisfies me like nothing else when I want this hit. It's hearty and homely and deeply comforting.

Japanese curry

This hearty and satisfying meal is just about every salaryman's favourite lunch in Tokyo. A great example of the fusion between Indian and Japanese cooking, it's more like a stew than a curry.

2 tablespoons light-flavoured oil
800g pork neck, cubed
30g butter
1 onion, thinly sliced
1 garlic clove, crushed with
    the flat of a knife
1 teaspoon grated ginger
2 tablespoons plain flour
1 tablespoon curry powder
1 litre chicken stock
2 carrots, peeled and
    cut into 3cm pieces
450g potatoes, peeled and cut
    into 4cm chunks
1 green apple, peeled and grated

Heat half the oil in a large saucepan over medium–high heat. Cook the pork in two batches for 4–5 minutes or until lightly browned all over. Repeat with the remaining oil and pork. Set aside.

Melt the butter in the same pan over low heat. Add the onion, garlic and ginger and cook, stirring occasionally, for 3–4 minutes or until soft. Add the flour and curry powder and cook for 1–2 minutes, stirring frequently. Gradually add the stock, whisking constantly. Add the pork, carrots, potatoes and apple and simmer for 2–2¼ hours until the potatoes break down and the meat is very tender. Serve with steamed rice. **Serves 4**

Stir-fried chilli pork

I love the astringent taste of the chillies against the crunch of nuts and the sweetness of the pork. Inspired by Asian street food, this should be served simply on top of plain steamed rice.

1 tablespoon soy sauce
2 tablespoons mirin
2 tablespoons hoisin sauce
2 teaspoons sesame oil
1 teaspoon dried chilli flakes
800g pork fillet, cut into 5mm-thin slices
3 tablespoons light-flavoured oil
4 garlic cloves, crushed with
    the flat of a knife
3 red chillies, cut in half lengthways,
    stalks left on and de-seeded
6 bulb spring onions, halved,
    or 1 small red onion, cut into wedges
1 tablespoon soy sauce
2 tablespoons granulated sugar
2 tablespoons roasted peanuts

Mix together the soy sauce, mirin, hoisin sauce, sesame oil and chilli flakes in a shallow dish. Add the pork, toss to coat and leave in the fridge to marinate for 15 minutes.

Heat a wok over high heat and add 1 tablespoon of the oil. When smoking, add half the pork and stir-fry for 1–2 minutes. Remove from the pan. Repeat this step.

Heat the remaining tablespoon of oil and add the garlic, chillies, 1 tablespoon water and the onions. Stir-fry for 3–4 minutes, covering the wok for 2 minutes. Add the soy sauce and sugar and return the pork to the wok. Cook for 1 minute. Garnish with the roasted peanuts and serve with steamed rice. **Serves 4**

Char sui-style barbecue pork ribs

I remember my mum once having a store cupboard disaster with a leaking bottle of red food colouring, which she would probably have used for making this kind of Peking-style ribs more appealing – or so she thought once upon a time. Ribs are becoming popular again as they're a cheap cut and a favourite with all the family.

4 garlic cloves, crushed with
    the flat of a knife
125ml soy sauce
100ml hoisin sauce
1 tablespoon honey
1 tablespoon sesame oil
1 teaspoon Chinese five spice powder
1kg boneless pork belly ribs

Combine the garlic, soy sauce, hoisin sauce, honey, sesame oil and five spice powder in a large bowl. Add the ribs, toss to coat and leave to marinate in the fridge for 10 minutes.

Preheat the oven to 160°C/gas mark 2–3. Line a deep roasting tray with foil, place a rack over the top and add 1cm water to the base of the tray. Place the pork on the rack and roast for 1 hour, brushing with marinade every 15 minutes. Turn the ribs over halfway through the cooking time. Lift the ribs onto a board and chop into pieces to serve. **Serves 4–6**

Sticky pork chops with peach chutney

I love the indulgent, retro mood of these chops, as it harks back to the seventies when glamour meant putting a bit of fruit with pretty much everything. The sweet peach chutney goes so well with the savouriness of the meat though, and tastes bang up-to-date.

3 tablespoons olive oil
1 small onion, grated
2 teaspoons granulated sugar
2 tablespoons rice vinegar
1 teaspoon ground cumin
½ teaspoon freshly ground black pepper
4 pork loin cutlets (about 220g each)
peach chutney (see recipe below)

Stir together the olive oil, onion, sugar, vinegar, cumin and pepper in a shallow dish. Add the pork and stir well. Cover and leave to marinate in the fridge for 30 minutes.

Preheat a barbecue or char-grill pan to high heat and brush lightly with olive oil. Cook the pork cutlets for 3–4 minutes on each side, or until cooked to your liking. Serve with the peach chutney (or a mango chutney if pressed for time). **Serves 4**

Peach chutney
2 teaspoons light-flavoured oil
½ red onion, diced
2 teaspoons mild curry powder
600g peaches, skinned, stoned and chopped
1 teaspoon julienned ginger
1 teaspoon soft brown sugar
1 tablespoon lime juice

Heat the oil in a saucepan over medium heat. Add the onion and cook for 2–3 minutes until starting to soften. Add the curry powder and cook for 30 seconds. Add the peaches, ginger, sugar and lime juice and stir until the sugar has dissolved. Simmer for 5 minutes or until the peaches soften. Leave to cool.

Japanese crumbed pork cutlet with cabbage salad

A fast-food favourite in Japan, these schnitzel-like cutlets are known there as 'tonkatsu'. Maisen, in Tokyo, which has been open since the sixties, is my favourite place to go for a tonkatsu fix, washed down with a cold Kirin beer. Just be sure to find Bulldog or, at the very least, HP sauce to eat it with as it's just not the same without!

¼ small green cabbage
8 pork escalopes (about 50g each)
110g plain flour
4 eggs
125ml milk
200g panko (Japanese dried breadcrumbs)
200ml light-flavoured oil
lemon wedges
tonkatsu sauce

Shred the cabbage finely and cover with iced water. Place the pork escalopes on a board and flatten with a meat mallet to a thin rectangular shape about 7cm x 8cm.

Place the flour in a bowl and season with sea salt and freshly ground black pepper. Whisk the eggs and milk together in a separate bowl. Spread the panko on a plate. Dust each escalope in the flour, shake off the excess, then dip in the egg mixture and coat in a layer of breadcrumbs. Repeat this process again so all the escalopes are crumbed twice.

Heat the oil in a large non-stick frying pan over medium heat. Place 2 escalopes in the pan in a single layer, being careful not to crowd them, and cook for 2–3 minutes on each side until golden brown. Remove from the pan, allowing any excess oil to drain off, then place on kitchen paper and keep warm. Repeat until all the escalopes are cooked.

Serve with the well-drained shredded cabbage, lemon wedges and tonkatsu sauce. **Serves 4**

Barbecued pork fillet with Vietnamese caramel sauce

Sweet and sticky caramel sauces are a great way to ease young or even cautious adult Western palettes into Asian flavours. A nice lean fillet of pork works perfectly and makes the dish lighter than if you were to use a fattier cut. Serve with lots of steamed greens and rice to soak up the sauce.

1 whole pork fillet (about 600g)
1 tablespoon fish sauce
1 teaspoon caster sugar
2 garlic cloves, crushed with
    the flat of a knife
Vietnamese caramel sauce
    (see recipe below)
handful coriander leaves

Cut the pork fillet in half crossways so it's easier to manage. Combine the fish sauce, sugar and garlic in a shallow dish. Add the pork and leave to marinate in the fridge for 10 minutes.

Lightly oil the char-grill or frying pan over medium–high heat and cook the pork for 3–4 minutes on each of the four sides or until just cooked. Rest for 5 minutes before slicing thickly. Dress with the caramel sauce and coriander leaves. **Serves 4**

Vietnamese caramel sauce
2 tablespoons soft brown sugar
2 tablespoons caster sugar
2 tablespoons light-flavoured oil
1½ tablespoons fish sauce
1½ tablespoons lime juice
1 long red chilli, finely sliced

Place the sugars and 2 tablespoons water in a small saucepan over low heat and cook until the sugars have dissolved. Increase the heat to medium and cook for 2 minutes or until reduced. Remove from the heat and allow to cool. Add the oil, fish sauce, lime juice and chilli and stir to combine.

Lamb & Beef

Whenever I have moments of thinking I could, and perhaps should, go vegetarian – I love the variety of vegetables so much this thought does cross my mind from time to time – I suddenly think how much I'd miss a perfectly cooked steak. While beef always feels that bit more indulgent to cook with, most of us saving it for a weekend or dinner party treat, it's also a lot more versatile than other types of meat, taking just as well to a long, slow braise as it does to a quick searing. There's also a much better, more flavourful quality to the beef available to us now, which stands up fantastically to Asian flavours. Unlike white meat or fish, beef can take deeper, richer sauces and marinades, making the dishes it's used in some of the most indulgent and satisfying. Having said that, some cuts need more attention than others: for example, it's no good using fillet steak if you're intending to braise it. So, as with your fishmonger, take the time to get to know your butcher and ask his advice about cooking techniques – he'll be the first to say that's what he's there for. I wasn't sure whether to include lamb in this book as it's not frequently used in Asia but I love its earthy quality in a rich Massaman curry and it works so well paired with the fruitiness of hoisin sauce that I couldn't resist.

Meatballs with tamarind

Every culture I can think of has ways to use up those odds and ends of meat that are made into mince, but you probably wouldn't have bought this book if it had been called '100 Ways With Mince'. These are a delicious Asian take on something most of us think of as being an American classic.

light-flavoured oil, to brush and drizzle
600g beef mince
1 tablespoon finely chopped ginger
3 tablespoons chopped coriander leaves
1 small red onion, grated
1 tablespoon soy sauce
tamarind glaze (see recipe below)

Preheat the oven to 240°C/gas mark 9 and brush a large roasting tray with oil. Put the mince, ginger, coriander leaves, grated onion and soy sauce in a large bowl and season with sea salt and freshly ground black pepper. Use your hands to mix the ingredients together until well combined, then roll heaped tablespoonfuls of the mixture into balls. Put the meatballs in the prepared tray, drizzle over a little extra oil and roast for 10 minutes.

Remove from the oven, pour the glaze over the meatballs and roast for a further 5 minutes. Repeat this step and roast for a further 2 minutes. Repeat once more. Serve with steamed rice and steamed Asian greens. **Serves 4–6 for a main meal**

Tamarind glaze
2 tablespoons light-flavoured oil
2 tablespoons tamarind paste
200ml honey
4 tablespoons lime juice
1 tablespoon soy sauce

Place the oil, tamarind paste, honey, 3 tablespoons water, lime juice and soy sauce in a small saucepan over medium heat. Bring to the boil then simmer for 4 minutes. Set aside.

Marinated Korean-style barbecued beef with miso slaw

This is my party-trick dish. You don't actually taste the kiwi fruit at all once it's cooked, the enzymes in it just do a great job of tenderising the meat, particularly skirt cuts. You can also use papaya, which has a similar effect. Serve in steak form or Korean-style as lettuce hand-rolls.

½ ripe kiwi fruit, peeled and mashed
3 tablespoons soy sauce
1 teaspoon sesame oil
2 garlic cloves, crushed with the flat of a knife
2 tablespoons soft brown sugar
1 tablespoon rice vinegar
3 steaks, 2.5cm thick (about 800g)
miso slaw (see recipe below)
Chinese chilli relish

Put the kiwi fruit, soy sauce, sesame oil, garlic, sugar and vinegar in a small bowl and stir to combine. Place this mixture with the steaks in a ziplock bag, seal the bag and massage the marinade into the steaks. Set aside to marinate in the fridge for 1–3 hours.

Preheat a barbecue or grill to high. Scrape the marinade off the steaks and grill for 3 minutes on either side. This will cook the steak to medium rare. Rest the steak for 5 minutes on a warm plate, then slice on the diagonal and serve with the miso slaw and Chinese chilli relish. **Serves 6**

Miso slaw
200g white cabbage, shredded
200g red cabbage, shredded
4 celery sticks, trimmed
    and cut into batons
1 red onion, thinly sliced
1 tablespoon rice vinegar
1 tablespoon caster sugar
1 tablespoon lemon juice
1 tablespoon white miso paste

Place the shredded cabbage, celery and onion in a large bowl. Combine the vinegar, sugar, lemon juice and miso paste in small bowl and stir until the sugar has dissolved. Pour over the vegetables and toss to combine. Serve immediately.

Black bean beef

This rolls off the tongue like, 'I'll have a number 53 please'. A classic Chinese takeaway favourite, it's a good way to put rump steak to use as it provides a bit of bite that stands up well against the saltiness of the black beans.

1 tablespoon mirin
2 tablespoons oyster sauce
1 teaspoon sesame oil
1 tablespoon cornflour
1 teaspoon caster sugar
350g rump steak, fat removed,
    thinly sliced
3 tablespoons light-flavoured oil
100g oyster mushrooms
1 red onion, cut into wedges
2 red chillies, quartered
    and de-seeded
50ml chicken stock
2 tablespoons soy sauce
60ml black bean sauce

Combine the mirin, 1 tablespoon of the oyster sauce, the sesame oil, cornflour and sugar in a shallow dish. Add the steak, toss to coat and set aside in the fridge to marinate for 5 minutes.

Heat a wok or frying pan over high heat. Add 1 tablespoon of the oil and stir-fry the steak in batches for about 1 minute or until well browned. Remove from the wok. Wipe the wok clean, heat another tablespoon of the oil, add the mushrooms and cook for 1 minute on each side or until lightly browned, turning the mushrooms carefully to avoid damaging them. Remove.

Add the last tablespoon of oil and stir-fry the onion and chillies for about 1 minute or until fragrant. Season with freshly ground black pepper. Return the steak to the wok with the stock, the remaining oyster sauce, soy sauce and black bean sauce. Stir-fry for 1–2 minutes or until the sauce reduces slightly. Add the mushrooms to warm them. Serve with steamed rice. **Serves 2**

Massaman lamb curry

The more serious foodies among us can be sticklers for staying true to a cuisine, but cultures have been crossing over and fusing flavours since the beginning of time. The name of this curry means 'Muslim', as the Thais used Muslim traders' spices to add depth and enrich its flavour.

3 teaspoons dried chilli flakes
1 tablespoon ground ginger
2 teaspoons cumin seeds
1 teaspoon white peppercorns
5 cardamom pods, cracked open and
   seeds removed (about ¼ teaspoon)
1 teaspoon sea salt
½ red onion, roughly chopped
6 garlic cloves, crushed with
   the flat of a knife
1 lemon grass stalk, white part only,
   roughly chopped
2 tablespoons chopped coriander roots
3 tablespoons light-flavoured oil
4 French-trimmed lamb shanks (about 1.3kg)
400ml tin coconut milk
1 tablespoon granulated sugar
1 tablespoon fish sauce
400g new potatoes, halved
1 tablespoon lime juice
2 tablespoons chopped roasted peanuts
large handful coriander leaves

Preheat the oven to 160°C/gas mark 2–3. Use a mortar and pestle to roughly pound the chilli flakes, ground ginger, cumin seeds, peppercorns, cardamom and sea salt. Blend the onion, garlic, lemon grass, coriander roots and 1 tablespoon of the oil in a blender as finely as possible, then stir in the spice mix. Alternatively, combine all the spices together in the blender.

Heat the remaining oil in a large flameproof casserole dish over medium–high heat. Add the lamb shanks and brown for 2 minutes on each side or until lightly browned all over. Remove from the dish. Add the curry paste mix and cook, stirring constantly, for 2 minutes or until fragrant. Return the lamb to the dish, add the coconut milk, 400ml water, sugar and fish sauce and bring to the boil. Remove the dish from the heat.

Add the potatoes and bake for 1¾–2 hours, turning the lamb 2–3 times while cooking, or until the meat is tender and falling off the bone and the sauce has reduced. Skim any fat off the surface and discard. Stir in the lime juice and scatter with peanuts. Serve with coriander leaves and steamed rice. **Serves 4**

Vietnamese steak with watercress

Inspired by a dish known as 'shaking beef' – simply because you cook it by shaking the pan – this seems to be having a moment again. It's one of the quicker and simpler beef dishes in this collection but still packs a punch. Serve on a bed of salad or greens.

600g sirloin steak
3 garlic cloves, roughly chopped
2 teaspoons granulated sugar
1 tablespoon light-flavoured oil
1 teaspoon sea salt
pinch ground white pepper
2 bunches asparagus,
    halved on an angle
large handful watercress, picked
½ tablespoon light-flavoured oil,
    for frying
3 tablespoons white wine
2 tablespoons soy sauce
2 teaspoons fish sauce
1 tablespoon soft butter

Cut the steak into 4cm x 4cm pieces. Use a mortar and pestle to crush the garlic with a pinch of sea salt. In a large bowl, toss the steak with the garlic, sugar, oil, salt and white pepper. Cover and set aside in the fridge to marinate for 1 hour. Meanwhile, blanch the asparagus in boiling water for 30 seconds, drain and refresh under cold running water. Arrange on a platter with the watercress and refrigerate until ready to serve.

Heat a large heavy-based frying pan over high heat and add the ½ tablespoon of oil. Cook the beef and its marinade, without touching, for 1 minute. Turn the beef and cook for another minute, then shake the pan for 30 seconds to cook the sides. Remove the beef from the pan and keep warm.

Add the white wine, soy sauce, fish sauce and butter and cook for another minute or until reduced and thickened. Place the beef on the prepared platter and dress with the sauce. **Serves 4**

Beef rendang

I'm afraid there aren't any short cuts in terms of how long you need to let this cook to reach its optimum level of sticky, dark richness. I think it was Charmaine Solomon's recipe I first tried and I've customised it according to my tastes over the years. So it's thanks to her that this is still a popular dish in my house.

2 red onions, roughly chopped
5 garlic cloves, peeled
2 tablespoons grated ginger
6 large red chillies, 3 de-seeded
    and roughly chopped,
    3 roughly chopped
3 lemon grass stalks, white part only,
    roughly chopped
3 tablespoons light-flavoured oil
2 tablespoons ground cumin
2 tablespoons ground coriander
2 teaspoons turmeric
2kg stewing steak, diced
400ml tin coconut milk
2 cinnamon sticks
1 tablespoon tamarind paste or lime juice
2 teaspoons sea salt
1 tablespoon soft brown sugar

Place the onion, garlic, ginger, chillies and lemon grass in a food processor and pulse to a paste. Heat the oil in a large heavy-based pan over medium heat. Add the paste and the cumin, coriander and turmeric and cook, stirring, for 2 minutes or until fragrant.

Add the stewing steak and cook over high heat for 4–5 minutes or until the beef is just sealed. Add the coconut milk, 400ml water, cinnamon sticks, tamarind paste, salt and sugar and bring to the boil. Reduce the heat and simmer, uncovered, for 2–2½ hours, stirring occasionally, or until the meat starts to break up and most of the liquid has evaporated. Serve with steamed rice and steamed Asian greens. **Serves 6 with leftovers**

Bibimbap

thick sirloin steak (about 250g)
1 tablespoon oyster sauce
1 small cucumber, very thinly
    sliced on a mandolin
1 teaspoon caster sugar
1 teaspoon rice wine vinegar
1 bunch spinach, stems removed
    at base of leaves
4 tablespoons light-flavoured oil
4 eggs
steamed rice
1 red pepper, cut in half,
    de-seeded and thinly sliced
Chinese chilli sauce
sesame seeds

Marinate the steak in the oyster sauce with a pinch of
sea salt and a pinch of ground white pepper for 15 minutes.
Meanwhile, prepare the vegetables while the steak is
marinating. Combine the cucumber slices with the sugar
and vinegar and set aside to marinate for 10 minutes. Pour
boiling water over the spinach leaves to wilt and drain well.

Heat a frying pan over medium–high heat. Add 1 tablespoon
of the oil and fry the steak for 2 minutes each side or until
slightly charred on the outside and rare inside. Set aside. Heat
the remaining oil in the pan over high heat. Break in 2 eggs,
on either side of the pan, and fry until the edge of the white is
bubbled and golden and the yolks are starting to set.
Remove to a plate and repeat with the remaining eggs.

To serve, thinly slice the meat. Place a portion of the steamed rice
in four bowls and top with the sliced beef, pickled cucumber,
spinach, red pepper, fried eggs and Chinese chilli sauce. Dress
with the sesame seeds. **Serves 4**

Crying tiger beef fillet with chilli dipping sauce

Along with Thai fishcakes and tom yum soup, this is one of those dishes that suddenly became really popular in the nineties. The idea behind the name is that the chilli content is so high it could make a tiger cry. But you can, of course, adjust it to whatever level you prefer.

2 tablespoons soy sauce
2 tablespoons fish sauce
1 tablespoon caster sugar
4 fillet steaks (about 200g each)
2 teaspoons light-flavoured oil
chilli dipping sauce (see recipe below)

Mix the soy sauce, fish sauce and sugar together in a shallow dish. Add the steaks, turn to coat and set aside in the fridge to marinate for 10–15 minutes.

Heat a large frying pan over high heat. When hot, add the oil and the drained steaks and sear for 2 minutes on each side for rare steak; allow an extra minute on each side for medium; or an extra 2–3 minutes on each side for well done. Transfer the steaks to a warm plate, cover loosely with foil and leave to rest for 2 minutes.

To serve, slice the steaks on the diagonal and serve with the dipping sauce and steamed Asian greens. **Serves 4**

Chilli dipping sauce
3 tablespoons fish sauce
3 tablespoons lime juice
1 tablespoon caster sugar
1 shallot, finely sliced
1 teaspoon dried chilli flakes
1 green chilli, finely chopped

Combine the fish sauce, lime juice, sugar, shallot, chilli flakes and green chilli in a small bowl. Set aside.

Lamb cutlets with satay sauce

Memories of the myriad varieties of Asian food served in Singapore have been swirling around in my head while writing this book. This dish was inspired by their mutton satay, which is one of the dishes I dream about the most.

2 teaspoons turmeric
½ teaspoon caster sugar
1 teaspoon sea salt
3 tablespoons light-flavoured oil
12 French-trimmed lamb cutlets
small handful coriander leaves
small handful mint leaves
finely sliced red onion
satay sauce (see recipe below)

Whisk the turmeric, sugar, sea salt and 2 tablespoons of the oil together in a shallow dish. Add the lamb cutlets and set aside in the fridge to marinate for 5 minutes.

Preheat a char-grill or griddle pan to medium–high heat and drizzle with the remaining tablespoon of oil. Grill the lamb cutlets for 3 minutes on each side or until crusty on the outside and pink in the middle. Dress with the herbs and onion and serve with the satay sauce. **Serves 4**

Satay sauce
250ml coconut cream
1 tablespoon red curry paste
100g coarsely chopped dry roasted peanuts
1 tablespoon soft brown sugar
1 tablespoon tamarind paste

Heat half the coconut cream over medium–high heat in a small saucepan for 6–7 minutes or until the cream is split and most of the water has evaporated. Reduce the heat to medium, add the curry paste and fry, stirring regularly, for 1–2 minutes or until fragrant and the paste loses its rawness.

Add the remaining coconut cream, peanuts, sugar and tamarind paste and cook for 2–3 minutes until thoroughly combined but still saucy. Set aside.

Noodles & Rice

The meat and vegetarian dishes are all very well but Asian food wouldn't exist without noodles and rice. They are the foundations of every meal, the yin to the yang of all those intense, punchy, complex flavours. These two carbohydrates are not just the plain, sensible partner – they can mingle and be a part of a multitude of dishes, from fragrant plates of pad Thai to steaming bowls of slippery pho noodle soups and umami-rich fried rice. No Asian culture would be without their noodle and rice dishes. These starches make what I love most about this style of cooking possible: the one-bowl meal, which becomes more and more of a good idea as our lives get increasingly busy. But as my own tastes develop I have grown to appreciate the simplicity of a bowl of classic cold Japanese soba noodles or a dish of aromatic ginger egg noodles with nothing more than some soy sauce and mirin on the side. Working with food every day, they're the ideal break for me when I want something completely pared down.

Hainanese chicken rice

Virtually the national dish of Singapore, this deliciously savoury one-bowl meal is a great family standby. Always popular with my girls, and any other waifs and strays around when I make it.

1.5kg chicken
½ bunch coriander, including roots
3 spring onions, roughly chopped
1 teaspoon black peppercorns
2 tablespoons sea salt
500g long-grain rice
1 tablespoon light-flavoured oil
1 tablespoon sesame oil
2 garlic cloves, crushed with
    the flat of a knife
1 tablespoon grated ginger
1 onion, chopped
2 small red chillies, chopped
2 tablespoons soy sauce
ginger and spring onion oil
    (see recipe below)

Place the chicken in a saucepan just large enough to fit snugly. Add the coriander, spring onion, peppercorns, salt and enough water to cover the chicken (about 4 litres). Bring to the boil. Reduce the heat to a simmer, cover the pan and simmer very gently for 25 minutes. Remove from the heat and leave the chicken in the covered pan for a further 40 minutes.

Wash the rice until the water runs clear. Heat the oils in a medium-sized saucepan over low heat. Add the garlic, ginger and onion and cook for 15 minutes or until the onion is soft. Add the rice and stir well to coat all the grains. Increase the heat to medium, add 1 litre of the chicken cooking liquid and bring to the boil. Reduce the heat to low, cover with a tight-fitting lid and cook for 15 minutes.

Remove the pan from the heat and leave to stand for 10 minutes. Do not lift the lid as it will interrupt the cooking process. Remove the chicken from the cooking liquid and cut into serving size pieces. Serve with the rice, the chopped chilli in the soy sauce and the ginger and spring onion oil. **Serves 4**

Ginger & spring onion oil
2 tablespoons finely chopped ginger
2 spring onions, finely sliced
1 teaspoon sea salt
4 tablespoons light-flavoured oil

Use a mortar and pestle to pound the ginger, spring onion and salt until bruised and broken up but not fine. Heat the oil in a small saucepan until very hot, pour over the ginger mixture and leave to cool. Set aside.

Simple egg noodle salad with peanut dressing

Noodle salads became a nineties staple and this is one of my favourites. It can also be used as a base for anything else you fancy adding: prawns, chicken, greens. This dish can be served cold, and it tastes even better the next day!

400g medium-width fresh egg noodles
1½ tablespoons honey
2 tablespoons smooth peanut butter
1 tablespoon lemon juice
1 tablespoon light-flavoured oil
1 tablespoon sesame oil
2 tablespoons soy sauce
1 tablespoon balsamic vinegar
1 carrot, peeled and shredded
1 red pepper, thinly sliced
100g roasted peanuts, chopped

Add the noodles to a large pan of lightly salted boiling water and cook for 3–4 minutes. Drain well. Whisk together the honey, peanut butter and lemon juice in a bowl, then gradually whisk in the oils, soy sauce and vinegar. Combine the dressing, noodles, carrot and red pepper, and dress with a sprinkling of peanuts. Serve warm or cold. **Serves 4 as a side dish**

Spring onion egg noodles with a ginger relish

When I first moved to Sydney from Melbourne, I became friends with a dynamic Malay-Chinese girl called Annie who wore denim cut-offs and drove a convertible jeep. On balmy Saturday evenings we'd buy barbecue pork from Chinatown, drive back with the roof down and music blaring, and make these noodles to keep us going for the night ahead.

400g thin fresh egg noodles
4 spring onions, finely sliced
    on the diagonal
2 tablespoons light-flavoured oil
2 tablespoons soy sauce
2 tablespoon rice vinegar
small bunch coriander
ginger relish (see recipe below)
Chinese barbecue pork (optional)

Prepare the egg noodles according to the instructions on the packet, cooking about 3 minutes less so they are al dente. Drain and rinse under cold running water.

Toss the noodles with the spring onion, oil, soy sauce and vinegar. Divide between four bowls and dress with the coriander. Serve with the ginger relish and Chinese barbecue pork if using. Delicious served warm or cold. **Serves 4 as a side dish**

Ginger relish
2 tablespoons finely grated ginger
2 spring onions, chopped
pinch sea salt
pinch ground white pepper
2 tablespoons light-flavoured oil

Use a mortar and pestle to lightly bruise the ginger, spring onion, salt and pepper. Heat the oil a small pan until smoking and pour over the ginger mixture in the mortar. Leave to cool.

Pad Thai

This noodle dish still seems to be everyone's guilty pleasure, often turned to as a way to absorb those last couple of cocktails during a big night out – Asia's equivalent of kebab, if you like. You'll be pleased to know that this version is healthier and super easy but just as tasty. Make sure the wok is as hot as you can get it to avoid ending up with a steamed, sludgy heap.

200g medium-width flat dried
   rice noodles
4 tablespoons light-flavoured oil
200g firm tofu, cut into 1.5cm dice
3 garlic cloves, crushed with
   the flat of a knife
1 red onion, sliced
2 eggs, beaten
1 tablespoon caster sugar
3 tablespoons fish sauce
3 tablespoons lime juice
4 spring onions, very finely sliced
100g bean sprouts
4 tablespoons roasted peanuts,
   roughly chopped
1 teaspoon dried chilli flakes
2 limes, cut into wedges
1 small cucumber, cut into chunks

Soak the noodles in hot water for 5 minutes to soften, drain well. Heat a wok over medium–high heat and add 2 tablespoons of the oil. Stir-fry the tofu for 3–4 minutes until browned all over. Season with sea salt and freshly ground black pepper and remove from the wok.

Add the remaining oil and stir-fry the garlic and red onion for 30 seconds or until the garlic is golden. Remove from the wok. Pour in the beaten eggs and season to taste. Cook, stirring once or twice, for 30 seconds. Add the drained noodles and toss to mix. Add the sugar, fish sauce and lime juice and stir-fry for 2–3 minutes. Return the garlic and onion to the pan, add the spring onion and bean sprouts. Return the tofu to the wok and toss to heat through.

Transfer to a serving platter, dress with the roasted peanuts and chilli flakes and serve with the lime wedges and cucumber.

Serves 2 as a main meal

I think I've passed my passion for fried rice on to my girls. I now have to make sure there's enough for lunchboxes the next day whenever I make it for dinner.

Prawn, leek & pea fried rice

This is basically a slightly posher version of special fried rice. I smile when I remember, as a teenager and a budding food snob, mocking my friends for ordering such an Anglo-sounding dish in a Chinese restaurant. I was secretly delighted when I later discovered that my Chinese friends eat it regularly at home.

3 tablespoons light-flavoured oil
1 leek, halved lengthways and
    thinly sliced on the diagonal
150g prawns, peeled, de-veined
    and chopped
3 eggs, lightly beaten
400g cooked long-grain white rice
150g peas, blanched in boiling water
    (or use frozen)
2 tablespoons oyster sauce
1 teaspoon caster sugar
1 teaspoon sea salt
1 tablespoon grated ginger
2 celery sticks, cut into 5cm batons
small handful coriander leaves

Place a wok or frying pan over high heat and add half the oil. Add the leek and prawns and stir-fry for 2–3 minutes or until the prawns turn pink. Remove from the wok. Add the eggs and scramble them until dry and golden brown.

Add the rice and stir-fry for 1 minute. Add the peas, oyster sauce, sugar, salt and ginger and stir-fry for 4–5 minutes. Transfer to two bowls and serve with the celery batons and a scattering of coriander leaves. **Serves 2**

Chilli fried rice with broccolini & tofu

Fried rice is my favourite comfort food fall-back. This one brings back memories of walking through the streets of Bangkok with the vinegary, spicy scent of rice dishes tossed around by street vendors filling the air. I'm sure you can actually become addicted to the smell alone.

2 tablespoons light-flavoured oil
3 tablespoons red curry paste
200g firm tofu, cut into small batons
200g broccolini, trimmed and sliced
    into 5cm lengths on the diagonal
740g cooked long-grain white rice
2 eggs, beaten
1 tablespoon fish sauce
1 teaspoon granulated sugar
8 spring onions, finely sliced
small handful coriander leaves
small handful basil leaves
cucumber batons
2 limes, cut into wedges

Place a wok or frying pan over high heat and add the oil. Cook the curry paste for 1 minute or until fragrant. Add the tofu and stir-fry for 3–4 minutes. Add the broccolini and stir-fry for 2 minutes.

Add the rice and toss to coat. Push the rice to the side of the wok, add the eggs and season with sea salt and freshly ground black pepper to taste. Stir the eggs until they start to set then mix with the fried rice. Add the fish sauce and sugar.

Serve scattered with spring onion and with the coriander, basil, cucumber batons and lime wedges on the side. **Serves 4**

Vietnamese rice noodles with sticky prawns

I love how this dish manages to be both clean tasting and sticky-sweet satisfying at the same time. It's the perfect meal for one or two when you want something special but super-quick, and you can spice it up with as little or as much chilli as you like. I like a lot!

250g rice vermicelli
2 tablespoons light-flavoured oil
16 large prawns, peeled and de-veined,
    tails intact
1 red onion, thinly sliced
3 garlic cloves,
    crushed with the flat of a knife
1 red chilli, finely chopped
2 tablespoons honey
2 tablespoons light soy sauce
4 tablespoons lime juice
small handful coriander leaves
1 cucumber, sliced
2 limes, cut into wedges

Place the rice vermicelli in a bowl and cover with boiling water. Soak for 6–7 minutes, then drain and rinse under cold water.

Place a wok or frying pan over high heat and add 1 tablespoon of the oil. Add the prawns and stir-fry for 2 minutes. Remove from the wok. Heat the remaining oil, then add the onion, garlic and chilli and stir-fry for 2 minutes. Return the prawns to the pan with the honey and soy sauce and stir-fry for 1 minute. Add the lime juice and remove from the heat.

Divide the noodles between four bowls. Top with the prawns, coriander and cucumber. Serve with lime wedges. **Serves 4**

Cold soba noodle salad with raw fish

There is a reverential attitude to soba noodles in Japan, above all other types of noodle. When 'first season' buckwheat soba arrive it's almost like a religious event. I love them because they're so healthy tasting and you never feel heavy after you've eaten them, especially when you have them cold.

270g dried soba noodles
1 green apple
1 avocado, peeled and stoned
2 teaspoons lime juice
400g very fresh white fleshy fish
small handful coriander leaves
2 limes, cut into wedges
salad dressing (see recipe below)
noodle dressing (see recipe below)

Cook the noodles according to the instructions on the packet. Drain and refresh in iced water, and drain well. Core the apple and cut into matchsticks and cut the avocado into chunks. Drizzle with the lime juice to prevent them going brown.

Divide the noodles between four serving bowls. Slice the fish into thin sashimi slices and arrange on small side plates. Place the apple, avocado and coriander on top with a few lime wedges. Drizzle with the salad dressing and serve the noodle dressing on the side in a dipping bowl. **Serves 4**

Salad dressing
4 tablespoons olive oil
2 tablespoons lime juice
½ teaspoon caster sugar
1 tablespoon soy sauce
1 teaspoon finely grated ginger

Whisk together all the ingredients in a small bowl. Set aside.

Noodle dressing
3 tablespoons light soy sauce
2 tablespoons mirin
1 tablespoon rice wine vinegar
2 teaspoons lime juice
1 spring onion, thinly sliced

Whisk together all the ingredients in a small bowl. Set aside.

Perfect rice

Rule one for anyone venturing into Asian cooking for the first time is not to be afraid of making perfect, fluffy rice. I used to think rice cookers were the foot spas of the kitchen in Asia and Australia until I discovered that they are actually very handy. Until I get around to buying one, however, here are three foolproof methods of getting rice right every time.

Steamed rice

400g long-grain white or jasmine rice
600ml water

Rinse the rice in a fine sieve, preferably until the water runs clear, and drain well. Put the rice and water in a large saucepan with a tight-fitting lid. Bring to the boil, put the lid on the pan, reduce the heat to low and cook for 12 minutes. Turn the heat off and leave to stand for 10 minutes. Do not remove the lid at any time during the cooking and standing process. Serve immediately. **Serves 4**

Brown rice

400g long-grain brown or basmati rice
1 litre water

Rinse the rice in a fine sieve, preferably until the water runs clear, and drain well. Put the rice and water in a large saucepan with a tight-fitting lid. Bring to the boil, put the lid on the pan, reduce the heat to low and cook for 30 minutes. Turn the heat off and leave to stand for 15 minutes. Do not remove the lid at any time during the cooking and standing process. Serve immediately. **Serves 4**

Coconut rice

400g long-grain white rice
500ml water
100ml coconut milk
1 teaspoon sea salt

Rinse the rice in a fine sieve, preferably until the water runs clear, and drain well. Put the rice, water, coconut milk and salt in a large saucepan with a tight-fitting lid. Bring to the boil, put the lid on the pan, reduce the heat to low and cook for 20 minutes. Turn the heat off and leave to stand for 5 minutes. Do not remove the lid at any time during the cooking and standing process. Serve immediately. **Serves 4**

Vegetables & Tofu

Kamakura in Japan is well-known for its incredible farmers' markets which have the most amazing variety of vegetables, all beautifully displayed. Being master horticulturalists, it doesn't surprise me that the Japanese are so adept at growing and preparing vegetables for the table – all of their dishes, even their garnishes, are like exquisite flower arrangements. I always feel so much healthier when I've spent time in Asia as I tend to eat a lot more vegetables – whether they're steamed, stir-fried, raw or pickled, they're never overcooked. I'm sure it was someone in Japan who looked at me strangely when I described someone as vegetarian. His reply was, 'You mean they eat a lot of vegetables?' It's only in the West that we tend to label our diets in such a way. Tofu, which tends to be a love or hate thing in the West, is a lot more widely used in the East. I've grown more and more fond of the stuff, enjoying its clean taste as a substitute for meat. One of Natalie's and my favourite simple suppers is a tofu omelette. Try it, you might surprise yourself!

Two ways with soy butter

The Japanese way of mixing soy and butter to finish a dish is a very clever, and undoubtedly fairly contemporary, trick. It adds a deliciously luxurious, savoury edge to whatever it's used to coat. Whether stirred through as many different types of mushroom you can find or baby new potatoes, it takes both vegetables to another level. Both are ideal accompaniments to a perfect steak – tofu or beef!

Potatoes with soy butter
50g butter, chopped
2 tablespoons soy sauce
1 tablespoon caster sugar
700g baby new potatoes,
    boiled and halved
1 spring onion, finely sliced

Add the butter, soy sauce and sugar to the hot, newly cooked and drained potatoes in a small saucepan. Cover and shake to coat, and season with freshly ground black pepper. Toss the potatoes over medium heat for about 5 minutes or until most of the liquid is absorbed. Serve immediately dressed with the spring onion. **Serves 4**

Mixed mushrooms with soy butter
2 tablespoons light-flavoured oil
300g mixed mushrooms,
    thickly sliced or halved
20g butter, chopped
1 tablespoon soy sauce

Heat the oil in a medium-sized saucepan over high heat. Add the mushrooms and cook for 3–5 minutes, putting in any larger meatier mushrooms first, before adding the more delicate mushrooms in the last 2 minutes. Add the butter and soy sauce and toss to coat. Serve immediately. **Serves 4**

Asian greens

This is a basic you will turn to time and time again. For me, a meal isn't complete without one or the other of these, or a crisp salad. And, of course, they are so healthy it takes the edge off any guilt you might be feeling about the main course.

Stir-fried Asian greens

1 tablespoon light-flavoured oil
3cm piece ginger, peeled
    and finely sliced
3 heads bok choy,
    quartered lengthways
1 tablespoon mirin
45ml chicken stock
½ teaspoon granulated sugar
1 teaspoon sesame oil

Heat a wok over high heat and add the oil. When hot, stir-fry the ginger until fragrant. Add the bok choy and cook for 1–2 minutes or until the leaves start to wilt. Add the mirin, chicken stock and sugar and season with sea salt to taste. Stir-fry for a further minute. Transfer to a serving plate, pour over the cooking juices and drizzle with sesame oil. **Serves 2**

Steamed Asian greens

2 tablespoons light-flavoured oil
large handful broccolini, trimmed
3 tablespoons chicken stock
2 tablespoons soy sauce
2 tablespoons mirin
1 tablespoon caster sugar
handful crispy shallots

Bring 1.25 litres water to the boil in a large saucepan and add 1 tablespoon of the oil. Blanch the broccolini for 2 minutes then drain. Transfer to a serving plate.

Heat the remaining oil in a wok over high heat. Add the stock, soy sauce, mirin and sugar and season with sea salt to taste. Bring to the boil and pour over the broccolini. Scatter with crispy shallots and serve. **Serves 2**

Butternut squash with a sweet sesame glaze

The sweet, autumnal flavours and inviting colours of this hearty dish make it a perfectly acceptable main course as well as an enticing side for a simple grill. Accompany with a portion of stir-fried greens and you can even get away with missing the gym for one night.

4 tablespoons soft brown sugar
2 tablespoons soy sauce
900g butternut squash, peeled, de-seeded and cut into 4cm pieces
1 tablespoon toasted sesame seeds

Place 200ml water, the sugar and soy sauce in a large saucepan and stir to dissolve the sugar. Bring to the boil over medium heat, add the butternut squash and cook for 10 minutes, stirring occasionally, or until the liquid has evaporated and the butternut squash is soft and sticky. Leave to cool slightly and serve scattered with the sesame seeds. **Serves 4**

Thai-style stir-fried butternut squash

Most single working chefs' fridges and pantries are notoriously understocked – a carton of milk is often the only thing in them, and that's usually seen better days. This is the great express lunch dish that Griff, my right-hand man at bills in Sydney came up with. The flavours go so well together and it's important to slightly catch the garlic in the pan so it imparts a lovely smoky flavour.

3 tablespoons light-flavoured oil
3 garlic cloves, bruised with the flat of a knife
2 long red chillies, sliced
400g peeled butternut squash, cut into thin wedges
2 eggs, lightly whisked
3 teaspoons fish sauce
2 teaspoons caster sugar
2 teaspoons lime juice
small handful basil leaves

Heat a wok over high heat and add the oil. Add the garlic and chilli and stir-fry for 2–3 minutes until golden. Remove from the oil with a slotted spoon.

Add the butternut squash to the wok and stir-fry for 2–3 minutes or until slightly charred and almost tender. Move to one side and pour the eggs into the other side of the wok. Stir-fry the eggs for 1–2 minutes or until cooked through. Add the fish sauce, sugar and lime juice and toss until the butternut squash is tender. Tear the basil leaves, add to the wok with the garlic and chilli and toss to combine. Serve immediately. **Serves 2**

Salt & pepper tofu with lemon soy dipping sauce

This is a great way to ease yourself into the idea of tofu – the crispy salt and pepper coating and spicy-sweet dipping sauce are a match made in heaven. It's also the ideal drinks snack for your vegetarian guests.

4 tablespoons plain flour
½ teaspoon Chinese five spice powder
500g silken tofu
600ml light-flavoured oil, for deep-frying
2 spring onions, thinly sliced
1 red chilli, sliced
lemon soy dipping sauce (see recipe below)
small handful coriander leaves

Season the flour generously with sea salt, freshly ground black pepper and the five spice powder. Cut the moist tofu into thick fingers and roll in the seasoned flour to coat.

Heat the oil in a deep saucepan over medium–high heat until hot. Drop the tofu into the oil and deep-fry for 3–4 minutes, tossing regularly, until golden all over. Remove and drain on kitchen paper. Fry the spring onion and chilli for 2–3 minutes or until starting to go golden. Remove and drain on kitchen paper.

Serve the tofu with the lemon soy dipping sauce and finish with the coriander leaves and the spring onion and chilli. **Serves 4**

Lemon soy dipping sauce
1½ tablespoons lime juice
1½ tablespoons lemon juice
3 tablespoons mirin
2 tablespoons light soy sauce

Put the lime and lemon juices and the mirin in a small saucepan. Bring to the boil then remove from the heat and set aside to cool. Stir in the soy sauce.

Barbecued corn with miso or chilli-coriander glaze

The earthiness of a whole cob of corn is made for the smoky flavour of the grill. A childhood favourite of mine and for many others, it works wonderfully as a starter or side, and the Asian-inspired glazes make it even more mouth watering.

miso glaze (see recipe below)
chilli-coriander glaze (see recipe below)
6 corn cobs, husks removed
1 tablespoon toasted sesame seeds
1 tablespoon thinly sliced spring onion

Prepare the glazes first and set aside. Preheat a covered barbecue to high heat.

Bring a large saucepan of water to the boil, add the corn and blanch for 2 minutes. Drain. Lightly oil the barbecue and cook the corn, with the barbecue lid down, for 10–12 minutes or until tender, turning occasionally.

To serve, brush the corn cobs with the miso or chilli-coriander glaze. Finish the miso-glazed cobs with the toasted sesame seeds and spring onion. **Serves 6**

Miso glaze
125g softened butter
3 tablespoons white miso paste
1 tablespoon soft brown sugar

Mix the butter, miso paste and sugar together in a bowl.

Chilli-coriander glaze
125g softened butter
1 chilli, de-seeded and finely chopped
2 tablespoons finely chopped coriander
1 tablespoon soft brown sugar

Mix the butter, chilli, coriander and sugar together in a bowl and season with sea salt and freshly ground black pepper to taste.

Asparagus, chilli & garlic stir-fry

One of the most elegant of all vegetables, bright green spears of asparagus are ubiquitous in Asian cooking, imparting their distinctive flavour which, although delicate, is never quite overpowered no matter how punchy the marinade.

2 tablespoons light-flavoured oil
6 garlic cloves, bruised with
    the flat of a knife
1 long red chilli, cut in half lengthways
2 bunches asparagus, ends trimmed,
    cut in half
3 teaspoons fish sauce
1½ teaspoons caster sugar
2 teaspoons lime juice

Heat a wok over high heat and add the oil. Add the garlic and chilli and stir-fry for 1 minute. Add the asparagus and stir-fry for another minute.

Add the fish sauce, sugar and 2 tablespoons water, cover and cook for 1 minute. Add the lime juice and toss. Serve immediately.
Serves 4 as a side dish

Green bean sambal

There's something about green beans that works so well with Asian food. They hold up really well both physically and in flavour against spices, and, for some reason, feel like one of the more sophisticated of side dishes to serve.

2 tablespoons light-flavoured oil
500g green beans
3 teaspoons sambal oelek (chilli paste)
1 red onion, cut into thin wedges
1 tablespoon lemon juice

Heat the oil in a medium-sized saucepan over medium heat. Add the beans and the sambal oelek and cook for 1–2 minutes. Add the onion and cook for a further minute. Remove from the heat and finish with the lemon juice. **Serves 6 as a side dish**

Miso aubergine

Usually served split into two halves in restaurants, this satisfyingly savoury dish is the kind of thing that tempts me to be vegetarian, or at least eat more of it. Here I've cut the aubergine into chunks and made more of the umami-rich sauce.

3 tablespoons light-flavoured oil
500g aubergine, chopped
2 tablespoons mirin
2 tablespoons soy sauce
1 tablespoon caster sugar
1 tablespoon white miso paste
4 spring onions, cut into 5cm batons

Heat a wok over medium–high heat. Add the oil and when hot, stir-fry the aubergine for 10 minutes. Mix the mirin, soy sauce, sugar and miso in a small bowl, add to the wok with the spring onion and stir-fry for 1 minute. Serve immediately. **Serves 4**

Tofu with soy sesame dressing

Tofu needs very little to make it delicious, and when I'm in the mood for something completely pared down with no frills, this is what I crave. It's especially good as a lazy but healthy summer lunch or supper.

400g firm tofu, halved
2 garlic cloves, chopped
½ teaspoon granulated sugar
4 tablespoons soy sauce
1 tablespoon sesame seeds, toasted
1 tablespoon sesame oil
1 tablespoon mirin
½ teaspoon dried chilli flakes
steamed brown rice (see page 199)
steamed Asian greens (see page 207)

Place the tofu in a saucepan of cold water and bring to a simmer over medium–low heat. Meanwhile, use a mortar and pestle to pound the garlic and sugar to a paste. Add the soy sauce, sesame seeds and oil, mirin and chilli flakes and stir to combine.

Place a portion of rice in two bowls and arrange the Asian greens on top. Remove the tofu from the water with a slotted spoon, place over the greens and drizzle with the dressing. **Serves 2**

Tofu & spring onion omelettes with soy-tomato sauce

In our first year of being parents, Natalie and I relied on tofu omelettes – they were our healthy version of fast food. The great thing about tofu is that it keeps, so there's no excuse not to have a packet or two in the fridge.

400g silken tofu, chopped
   and lightly mashed with a fork
6 eggs, beaten
8 spring onions, finely chopped
light-flavoured oil, for frying
soy-tomato sauce (see recipe below)
lemon wedges
small handful coriander leaves

Mix the tofu with the eggs and spring onion. Season with sea salt and freshly ground black pepper to taste. Heat a little oil in a non-stick frying pan over medium–high heat. Using a small ladle of egg mixture for each omelette, cook saucer-size omelettes for 1–2 minutes on each side or until just set. Serve with the soy-tomato sauce, lemon wedges and coriander leaves. **Serves 4**

Soy-tomato sauce

1 tablespoon light-flavoured oil
1 onion, sliced
2 garlic cloves, crushed with
   the flat of a knife
3 tomatoes, finely chopped
3 tablespoons soy sauce
1 tablespoon granulated sugar
pinch dried chilli flakes (optional)

Heat the oil in a small saucepan over medium–low heat. Add the onion and cook for 3–5 minutes or until soft. Add the garlic and cook for 1 minute. Add the tomato, bring to the boil and cook for 5 minutes or until soft. Add the soy sauce, sugar and chilli flakes if using, and bring to the boil. Reduce the heat to a simmer and cook a further 5 minutes or until the sauce has thickened slightly.

Desserts

Although desserts aren't the first thing that come to mind when I think of Asian food, I always welcome something refreshingly fruity and palate cleansing at the end of a soy-rich meal and, as with their savoury dishes, they seem to have a knack for balancing flavours that you wouldn't immediately think went together, like pineapple and chilli.I also love how they like to add an edge to their puddings – and way before it became the 'foodie' thing to do – by using a little salt in things like caramel sauce and sticky rice. There's a restaurant called Longrain in Sydney that does amazing tasting plates of sticky black rice and coconut caramel custard with grilled banana, with the unmistakable savoury hit lurking in there somewhere, which always get my taste buds going. I am also a huge fan of the extraordinary ice cream they make in Japan. The Italians will always be the masters of gelati, but Japan is forever reaching new heights of sophistication with flavours like yuzu, Earl Grey and black sesame – although I must admit I'm still struggling to appreciate avocado and tomato. Whether you prefer a zingy citrus hit or something gooey, caramelised and slightly salty, as much as you might pretend you're not a dessert person, Asian puddings are hard to resist.

It's hard to improve on a fresh mango mountain (the name my kids gave to mango hedgehogs) but sticky rice is the one thing that make this luscious fruit an even more delectable dessert.

Mango & sticky rice

Every backpacker returns from Thailand dreaming of this magic dish. The sweet-saltiness of the coconut rice and soft, juicy mango are a winning combination. The best I've ever tasted was at David Thompson's Sydney restaurant, Sailor's Thai.

300g arborio rice
400ml tin coconut milk
½ teaspoon sea salt
230g soft brown sugar
1–2 mangoes, peeled, stoned and sliced

Place the rice, coconut milk, salt and 750ml water in a medium-sized saucepan. Bring to the boil over medium–high heat then reduce the heat to a simmer and cook, stirring regularly, for 15–20 minutes or until the rice is tender. Remove the pan from the heat and stir in half of the sugar.

For the syrup, combine the remaining sugar and 60ml water in a small saucepan. Simmer, stirring, over medium–high heat for 3–4 minutes or until syrupy. Spoon over the rice and serve with the mango slices. **Serves 4–6**

Chinese custard tarts

*In China these little sweets
are most commonly found in
dim sum restraurants and
are inspired by Portuguese
custard tarts, when they
actually use a shorter pastry
than the flaky sort traditionally
used in the European version.
For anyone afraid of making
stovetop custard you'll be
pleased to know that the oven
does all the work for you!
For larger tarts you can make
this in an 8-hole 125ml muffin
tin. Increase the baking time
to 20–25 minutes.*

5 egg yolks
80g caster sugar
125ml single cream
125ml milk
2 teaspoons vanilla extract
1 sheet good-quality ready-rolled puff pastry

Preheat the oven to 200°C/gas mark 6. Lightly grease a 12-hole
80ml muffin tin. Put the egg yolks, sugar, cream, milk and
vanilla extract in a large bowl and beat until combined. Set aside.

Cut the pastry sheet in half, put one half on top of the other
and set aside for 5 minutes. Roll up the pastry tightly from the
short end and cut the pastry log into 12 x 1cm rounds. Lay
each pastry round on a lightly floured surface and use a rolling
pin to roll out until each is 10cm in diameter.

Press the pastry rounds into the prepared muffin tin. Spoon
the custard mixture into the pastry cases and bake for
18–20 minutes or until both the pastry and custard are golden.
Leave the tarts in the tin for 5 minutes before transferring
to a wire rack to cool. **Makes 12**

Passion fruit granita

In Australia, passion fruit vines grow like weeds in just about everyone's backyard so there's no shortage of them for a recipe like this. You will need about 9–12 passion fruit or you can use frozen pulp. Intensely zingy, this frozen granita makes the perfect palate cleanser. My tip is to whiz the seeds in a blender then strain through a sieve to get all the pulp out.

230g caster sugar
250ml passion fruit pulp,
    strained to make 125ml juice
1 tablespoon lime juice
coconut milk
pulp from 2 passion fruit, extra

Combine the sugar and 625ml water in a saucepan and stir over medium heat until the sugar has dissolved. Set aside to cool. Add the strained passion fruit juice and lime juice and stir to combine. Pour the liquid into a shallow metal tray and freeze for 2 hours or until starting to set around the edges.

Use a fork to break up the ice crystals and return the tray to the freezer. Repeat this step after each hour for another 2–3 hours or until the granita has frozen into large ice crystals.

To serve, spoon the granita into bowls, pour over a little coconut milk and the extra passion fruit pulp. **Serves 4**

Fruit salad with lemon grass & lime syrup

This is a fancier version of the little dishes of fresh fruit served in Chinese restaurants at the end of a meal. Palate-cleansing and refreshing, fruit salad is one of those things that's always worth the effort to make. I have such a weakness for syrupy, tinned lychees that I've been known to pretend that I can't find the fresh ones.

80ml fresh orange juice
40ml fresh lemon juice
20ml fresh lime juice
140g granulated sugar
2 lemon grass stalks, cut into
    5cm lengths and lightly crushed
1 tablespoon finely julienned ginger
2 ripe mangoes, skin removed, stoned
    and cut into chunks
1 small papaya, skin removed and
    cut into chunks
12 lychees, peeled, halved and stoned

Strain the fruit juices and combine with the sugar and lemon grass in a saucepan over medium heat. Stir to dissolve the sugar. Increase the heat to high and bring to the boil, then reduce the heat and leave to simmer for 10 minutes or until slightly reduced and syrupy. Strain, if desired, then stir in the ginger and leave to cool.

Place the mangoes, papaya and lychees on a serving plate and drizzle with the syrup to serve. **Serves 4**

Petit fours

These little after-dinner treats are ideal when you don't want to make a proper pudding and are equally an imaginative dinner party gift. The truffles were inspired by the delicious coconut chocolate bars that a shop called Melt in London make, which are like a more sophisticated version of that old favourite, the Bounty bar.

Ginger fudge

185g soft brown sugar
460g caster sugar
200ml single cream
150ml condensed milk
100g unsalted butter, chopped
pinch sea salt
3 pieces stem ginger in syrup, drained
 and finely chopped or 1½ tablespoons
 finely chopped glacé ginger

Lightly grease a 20cm square cake tin. Place the sugars, cream, condensed milk, butter and salt in a large saucepan. Cook over low heat, stirring constantly, until the sugar dissolves.

Bring to the boil and, stirring constantly, continue to boil until the mixture forms a thick syrup which reaches 116°C (soft ball stage) on a candy thermometer – this will take about 15 minutes. Alternatively, test the temperature by dropping some syrup into a bowl of iced water; the syrup should mould into a ball in the water but lose shape once out of the water.

Remove the pan from the heat and set aside for 30 minutes. Add the ginger and, with a wooden spoon, beat the mixture until it thickens. Pour into the prepared tin and set aside to cool completely before cutting into rough squares with a knife warmed in hot water. **Makes 42 x 3cm pieces**

Coconut truffles

200g dark chocolate, finely chopped
125ml single cream
icing sugar, to dust
fresh coconut, grated

Line a baking tray with baking paper or cling film. Put the chocolate in a large heatproof bowl. Heat the cream to scalding point in a small saucepan then quickly pour it over the chocolate. Mix thoroughly until all the chocolate has melted and the mixture is smooth. Set aside to cool, then refrigerate for about 30 minutes.

When the mixture is set, dust your hands with icing sugar to prevent the chocolate sticking and roll the mixture into small balls. Immediately roll the truffles in the grated coconut and place them on the baking tray. Refrigerate to set for a further 30 minutes before serving. **Makes 18**

Lime jelly with lychees

Jelly is having a moment right now with 'jellymongers', such as with the British duo Bompass & Parr, lending a hand in reviving its wobbly popularity. Maybe everyone's eating too much and needs a break from all those rich flavours – or we're simply enjoying reliving our childhoods.

1 tablespoon (12g) powdered gelatine
240g caster sugar
grated zest 2 limes
100ml lime juice (about 4 limes)
80ml vodka (optional)
handful fresh lychees, peeled and stoned

Pour 200ml water (if using the vodka use 120ml) into a small saucepan. Gradually sprinkle the gelatine over and leave to soak for 5 minutes. Stir in the sugar, place the pan over low heat and continue stirring until the gelatine and sugar have dissolved. Do not allow to boil. Set aside to cool for 5 minutes.

Add the lime zest and juice and the vodka if using. Strain through a fine sieve and pour into 4 x 125ml glasses and refrigerate for 4 hours or until set. Serve the individual jellies with the lychees or other tropical fruit of your choice. **Serves 4**

Mango pudding

As much as I believe in cheating and using store cupboard standbys from time to time, I've never been a fan of the evaporated milk traditionally used to make this dim sum restaurant perennial. My version is made with yoghurt and a little cream, which gives it a much fresher flavour – almost lassi like.

2 gelatine leaves (4.5g) or
  1½ teaspoons powdered gelatine
3 tablespoons single cream
115g caster sugar
375g mango flesh, puréed
  (about 1–2 mangoes)
3 tablespoons natural yoghurt
1½ teaspoons lime juice
1 mango, peeled and diced

Soak the gelatine leaves in cold water or gradually sprinkle the powder over 1½ tablespoons water in a medium-sized bowl. Place the cream, sugar and soaked gelatine in a small saucepan over medium heat and stir until the sugar has dissolved. Remove from the heat and allow to cool for 2 minutes.

Stir in the mango purée, yoghurt and lime juice and whisk gently to combine. Pour the mixture into four 180ml bowls, cover and refrigerate for 4 hours to set. Serve the individual puddings topped with the diced mango. **Serves 4**

Coconut & lime slice

There's something nicely old-fashioned about coconut in a cake or cookie, and although these probably aren't authentically Asian, they work so well with a fragrant cup of jasmine tea and perhaps some chunks of fresh watermelon, after a flavourful dinner.

Vanilla base

150g unsalted butter,
 at room temperature
110g caster sugar
1 teaspoon vanilla extract
225g plain flour
40g cornflour
160g lime marmalade

Coconut & lime filling

3 eggs
100g caster sugar
80g shredded coconut
30g plain flour
200ml single cream
125ml coconut milk
grated zest 2 limes
60ml lime juice

Preheat the oven to 180°C/gas mark 4. Lightly grease a 26cm x 16cm shallow baking tin and line the base and sides with baking paper.

To make the base, beat the butter, sugar and vanilla extract with electric beaters until pale and creamy. Sift the flour and cornflour into the mixing bowl and beat on low speed until just mixed to a crumbly consistency. Press into the prepared tin and bake for 12–15 minutes or until light golden. Remove from the oven and leave to cool for 10 minutes. When cool, spread evenly with the lime marmalade.

To make the filling, place the eggs and sugar in a bowl and whisk until pale. Add the shredded coconut, flour, cream, coconut milk, lime zest and juice and stir to combine. Carefully pour the filling over the pastry base. Bake for 35–40 minutes or until golden. Remove from the oven and allow to cool completely in the tin before cutting into squares. **Makes 24 squares**

Banana batter cake with coconut caramel sauce

This Asian variation on sticky toffee pudding is popular with just about everyone. One of those desserts that you offer to share with someone and then wish you had the whole plate to yourself. Definitely worth saving room for.

150g self-raising flour
115g caster sugar
pinch sea salt
3 bananas, 1 mashed,
    2 halved lengthways
1 egg
250ml milk
100g butter, melted and cooled
2 teaspoons vanilla extract
140g light brown sugar
coconut milk

Preheat the oven to 180°C/gas mark 4. Lightly grease a 20cm square x 3cm high baking tray.

Combine the flour, caster sugar and salt in a large bowl and stir to combine. Whisk together the mashed banana, egg, milk, butter and vanilla extract. Add the wet ingredients to the dry ingredients and stir until smooth and combined. Pour into the prepared tray and decorate with lines of banana. Sprinkle with the brown sugar and pour 125ml water over the top.

Place in the oven and bake for 25–30 minutes or until a skewer inserted into the centre comes out clean. Set aside to cool slightly. Serve with coconut milk. **Serves 4**

Mandarin crème brûlée

In the last fifteen years I think I've seen every variation of crème brûlée possible on restaurant menus around the world – I'm surprised I haven't come across a beetroot one! Mandarin is a lovely foil to the sweetness of the vanilla flavour of the baked cream.

600ml double cream
4 wide strips mandarin peel,
    white pith removed
6 egg yolks
65g caster sugar
extra caster sugar, to sprinkle

Preheat the oven to 140°C/gas mark 1. Place the cream and mandarin peel in a saucepan over medium heat and bring to almost boiling point. Remove, cover and set aside to infuse for 15 minutes.

Whisk the egg yolks and caster sugar together in a large bowl until pale. Remove the mandarin peel from the cream and discard. Add the hot cream to the egg mixture and whisk until well combined. Using a large spoon, scoop off any excess foam on the surface of the mixture and discard.

Place a folded tea towel in the base of a large deep roasting tray. Place 6 x 150ml ovenproof ramekins in the tray. Strain the mixture into a pouring jug and then divide equally between the ramekins. Pour enough boiling water in the base of the tray to come halfway up the sides of the ramekins, then loosely cover the tray with foil.

Bake for 55–60 minutes or until the custards still have a slight wobble in the centre. Carefully remove the ramekins from their water bath and set aside to cool. Cover with cling film and refrigerate overnight.

When ready to serve, sprinkle about 2 teaspoons caster sugar over the top of each custard and spread to cover with the back of a spoon. Use a blowtorch to melt the sugar evenly until it caramelises then allow to cool. Alternatively, preheat a grill on high, place the custards in a tray filled with ice cubes (to prevent them melting) and grill for 3–4 minutes or until the sugar dissolves and caramelises. **Serves 6**

INDEX

FOR NATALIE, EDIE, INÈS AND BUNNY

A book is the sum of many parts and I would like to extend a massive and heartfelt thank you to all who made this book a reality, taking the mad journey with me: Fran Caratti, Griff Pamment, Toby Anderson, Tanya Freymundt, Celeste Wilde and the bills team for working hard and consistently day-in day-out; Rick McKenna for getting us started; Erika for encouraging us to go places we usually wouldn't (Gilligan's Island, anyone?); Mikkel for his mad energy and enthusiasm and pushing himself even further; Mary for her calm, measured approach and beautiful design; Glenda for massaging my words and making them work; Kathy for her organisation and care and managing the ever-important testing; Victoria for being our rock and making sense of it all; Nick for his commitment, enormous effort and patience; Sacha for her good humour and hard work; Tibbie Chiu and Megan Petersen for their last-minute much-needed assistance; Jane Price for her guidance and experience, we're so sorry you couldn't make it to the end with us; Summer Litchfield for always being a joy and having a laugh, more important than you might imagine; Paul Aikman for interpreting our instructions and realising our striking images; Edie, Inès and Bunny for their patience, their extraordinary sense of adventure and trying food all around the world, including a seven-course tofu meal in Tokyo; and Nats for pushing me when I don't think I can be pushed any more, and gluing us crazy creatives together to form a complete whole that in the end makes sense. Thank you to Alison and Jane for your belief in me and my work, Ian, Clare and Mark for taking my book out into the world and Helen for your ongoing encouragement.

Creative Director: Erika Oliveira
Photographer: Mikkel Vang
Designer: Mary Libro, Feeder
Editor: Glenda Downing
Contributing editors: Summer Litchfield, Jane Price
Food editor: Kathy Knudsen
Food preparation: Nick Banbury, Griff Pamment, Sacha Seear
Recipe testing: Nick Banbury, Alison Adams, Cynthia Black, Wendy Brodhurst, Sydney Pemberton, Kerrie Sun, Bronwen Warden
Production for photography: Ate Consulting Pte Ltd (Singapore), Sheridan Nilsson, Celeste Wilde
Merchandising: Geraldine Muñoz, Sheridan Nilsson
Production Manager: Victoria Jefferys
Prepress: Paul Aikman, Graphic Print Group
Producer: Natalie Elliott

For Quadrille:
Publishing Director: Jane O'Shea
Creative Director: Helen Lewis
Production: Vincent Smith, Aysun Hughes

The publisher, Bill Granger and the creative team would like to sincerely thank the following for their generosity in assistance with homewares and clothes: Virgine Batterson, China Squirrel, Ici et La, Jac and Jack, Sandy Lockwood, Major and Tom, Mamapapa, Mao and More, Mud Australia and ToTT Store (Singapore).

All spoon measures are level unless otherwise stated and 1 tablespoon equals 15ml.

Cooking temperatures and times relate to conventional ovens. If you are using a fan-assisted oven, set the oven temperature 20 degrees or 1 Gas Mark lower. For baking, I recommend a conventional oven rather than a fan-assisted oven.

Anyone who is pregnant or in a vulnerable health group should consult their doctor regarding eating raw or lightly cooked eggs.

This edition first published in 2017 by
Quadrille Publishing Limited
Pentagon House, 52-54 Southwark Street,
London, SE1 1UN
www.quadrille.co.uk

Text © 2011 William Granger
Photography © 2011 Mikkel Vang
Design and layout © 2011 bills Licensing Pty Limited

Cataloguing in Publication Data: a catalogue record for this book is available from the British Library.

ISBN 978 184949 957 6

Printed in China

www.bills.com.au